I0424854

# Undefeated

# Conquer Trauma and Reclaim Your Life

by
Kang Hatanosen

# Undefeated: Conquer Trauma and Reclaim Your Life – About the Book

Triumph Over Adversity: Transcend Your Trauma and Reclaim Your Life

Immerse yourself in the transformative journey from struggle to strength with **"Undefeated: Conquer Trauma and Reclaim Your Life"**. This groundbreaking book offers a beacon of hope to those grappling with the aftermath of trauma and a roadmap to reclaim their lives.

If you've experienced trauma, you may feel like your life is defined by your tumultuous past. However, *'Undefeated'* is a testament to the fact that you are not your trauma. With this book, you'll gain a profound understanding of the impact of trauma, learning how to recognize its manifestations in your life and how it shapes your experiences.

**You're not alone in your journey to healing.** 'Undefeated' shares the courageous stories of survivors who've wrestled with trauma and emerged victorious. Their tales reflect resilience, healing, and the reclaiming of their lives - an indomitable testament to the human spirit.

But this book is more than inspirational; it's actionable. It presents you with proven psychological techniques - from Cognitive Behavioral Therapy to Eye Movement Desensitization and Reprocessing - allowing you to actively participate in your healing journey. You'll also discover self-help strategies like journaling and mindfulness which can complement formal therapies.

Attaining survival is just part of the process; thriving is the ultimate goal. The latter parts of 'Undefeated' focuses on rebuilding your life post-trauma - fostering trust, building healthy relationships, improving self-image, and returning to professional life.

The book concludes by providing essential resources and a compendium of interventions designed to support your continued healing process.

The battle may be tough, but 'Undefeated' encourages you to not just endure but to emerge victorious - a true survivor, resilient, and in control. Allow this book to guide you on your journey to becoming **undefeated**.

## Table of Contents

# Introduction

Within each of us, there's a story of resilience waiting to be written. An untold narrative of overcoming, conquest, and triumph. Tales of defeating our monsters, both internal and external, and emerging stronger, fiercer, and unstoppable.

This book is about trauma. But more significantly, it's about rising from the grips of pain and rebirth. It is about resilience, growth, strength, and triumph. This isn't a tale of sadness or despair but an account of how we, as humans, can overcome our somber adversities and reclaim our lives.

Everyone, at some point, experiences something that overturns their world. Some events leave an indelible mark on our lives, morphing us into different individuals, often against our will. These happenings are our traumas—the deep-seated pains that mold us, shape us, often confining us in their dark wraps.

Everybody's trauma is unique and deeply personal. It may be a terrible accident, an abusive relationship, loss of a loved one, surviving a natural disaster, or a profound personal violation. Regrettably, some are born into trauma, carrying the burden of intergenerational pain and suffering.

However, scars of the past need not define our future. This book is a testament to the belief that we can transcend life's worst moments. This resource guides you to acknowledge the torment that has churned your life, understand how it has shaped you, and ultimately reveal the path to overcoming the pain and reclaiming your life.

By exploring real-life experiences of survivors and learning from their exceptional resolve and strength, you can gain invaluable insights. Their stories are not just examples of fortitude but can serve nearly as blueprints for your own journey to healing.

Our exploration of trauma does not only dwell on the emotional perspective. We also dive into the physical implications, long-term impacts, and the silent epidemic that trauma creates. This holistic picture aims to present a comprehensive view of trauma, fostering better understanding, empathy, and healing.

Just as any wound requires proper treatment to heal, deep-seated trauma needs the right strategies and techniques for recovery. This book offers not only an insight into formal therapy methods but also delves into self-help techniques that foster healing.

From techniques like Cognitive Behavioral Therapy and Eye Movement Desensitization and Reprocessing, to simpler remedies like mindfulness and journaling, we offer proven strategies that can guide your path to recovery.

Yet the journey does not end with healing. Rebuilding life after trauma is another crucial facet of this journey. We address how to rebuild trust, discover healthy relationships, return to professional life, and most importantly, heal your self-image.

But how do you continue to stay undefeated once you've conquered your trauma? Our final sections focus on cultivating resilience. This chapter acts as a guide on how to turn healing into thriving, ensuring that you grow beyond survival. It includes practical steps for prioritizing self-care, nourishing connections, and fostering gratitude and positivity.

To reinforce your journey, we have provided numerous trauma-informed interventions and resources. These dedicated sections include activities, exercises and assignments, and a memoir of healing from complex trauma to inspire and guide you throughout your healing journey.
However, remember that this book is not a replacement for any professional help that may be necessary. It functions as a guide, providing resources and helping you understand and cope with trauma, but it is always important to seek professional guidance when needed.

It is our hope that this book will help illuminate your path, empower you to take the first steps towards healing, and inspire you to reclaim your life, transforming from victim to triumphant survivor. The journey may be arduous, but remember, your spirit is stronger, and you are not alone.

# Chapter 1: Understanding Trauma

Stemming from an etymologically Greek background, 'Trauma' fundamentally means 'wound' and it's a term that hails heavily-loaded--an event or circumstance that yanks the carpet out from under you, leaving your reality skewed, your worldview changed, and yourself markedly different. Trauma, though, isn't an easy subject to pin down. It's not a one-size-fits-all kind of umbrella term; it's highly individual and it varies tremendously from person to person, spanning a gamut from emotional to physical to inherited family trauma and everything in between. Hence, your first step on the path to recovery is understanding what trauma is and what it may look like in your life. You might ask, "Is it a singular catastrophic event? A prolonged exposure to intense stress? Or could it be something I've inherited from generations past?" The truth is, it may well be any, or a combination of, these things. Recognizing trauma, correctly identifying it in your life, is no simple task given the misconceptions that abound. Trauma is not simply a by-product of not being 'tough enough', nor is it a sign of weakness or inability. It's a deeply held wound that exerts far-reaching implications on who we are; manifestations of unfaced pain, un-shed tears, and unheard stories. So, let's embark on this journey of understanding trauma, not just as a sterile definition, but as a reality that may have been subtly— or not so subtly influencing your world. Together, we'll explore defining trauma, identifying its presence in your life, understanding inherited family trauma, and dispelling common misconceptions about it. All with the sole intention of arming you with the knowledge needed to take back the reins and truly start the process of healing. The journey may tax you, but the rewards are invaluable--after all, understanding is the first step toward reclaiming your life.

# Defining Trauma

The term trauma is often thrown around lightly in our everyday conversations, but its true definition goes beyond simple upsetting experiences. Trauma is a complex and layered phenomenon, carrying significant emotional weight. It's crucial to remember that trauma is based on an individual's perception and capacity to cope, and what might traumatize one person might not necessarily have the same impact on another.

All trauma, regardless of its nature, triggers a state of distress when an individual's safety or life is threatened. This threat could be physical or emotional, real or perceived. A traumatic event, therefore, is any situation that elicits this overwhelming fear and helplessness.

The American Psychological Association defines trauma as the emotional response to a terrible event such as an accident, rape, or disaster. Immediately after the event, shock and denial are common. However, longer-term reactions might involve unpredictable emotions, flashbacks, strained relationships, and even physical symptoms.

It's vital to note, experiencing trauma does not automatically lead to a disorder, but it can trigger symptoms and conditions such as post-traumatic stress disorder (PTSD), acute stress disorder, and more. A traumatic event can shake your world and make you question your safety and sense of self. With time and effective coping skills, most people recover from trauma, but some may require professional intervention.

Trauma can be broken down into different categories. 'Acute trauma' is the result of a single traumatic event—a car crash or an episode of violence. 'Chronic trauma' results from prolonged and repeated exposure to highly stressful situations. Examples include domestic violence, child neglect or abuse, or living in a war-stricken region. 'Complex trauma' describes simultaneous or sequential traumatic experiences, often invasive and interpersonal, occurring within specific time periods or particular contexts and relationships. It could involve premeditated, deliberate acts such as severe, repetitive physical or sexual abuse.

On the other hand, 'secondary trauma,' sometimes referred to as vicarious trauma, is induced by hearing about or witnessing a traumatic event involving someone else. This type of trauma can affect caregivers, emergency personnel, therapists, or even friends and family members of trauma survivors. It reminds us that trauma can permeate our emotional barriers and deeply affect even those indirectly involved.

*Historical trauma* or *generational trauma* is another type of trauma that affects entire communities or groups of people. This refers to the cumulative emotional harm experienced over several generations following massive group trauma incidents. Consider the profound effects on communities who have experienced penetrative, large-scale events such as war, genocide, slavery, or colonization.

No matter the specific type, all forms of trauma can lead to lasting psychological and physiological changes. These alternations may impact a person's emotions, behavior, cognition, identity, and relationships. It's essential to not underestimate the ripple effects trauma can have on an individual's life, even years after the triggering event.

So what makes an event traumatic? Truthfully, it's not about the event itself, but rather how a person perceives and responds to it. The same event can impact different people in very different ways. One person may walk away from a car accident seemingly unscathed, while another person may develop PTSD from the same incident. It all boils down to one's subjective appeal, and it's vital to avoid comparison or belittling one's sensitivity to trauma.

Moving on, let's briefly delve into the concept of inescapability in trauma. A traumatic event often involves a sense of helplessness, highlighting the individual's inability to escape the situation. This overwhelming realization that the situation is unmanageable can be even more distressing than the event itself.

Lastly, we cannot discuss trauma without addressing the body's natural reaction to it- the fight, flight, or freeze response. This primal, automatic response prepares the body to either combat the threat, escape from it, or tense up and play dead in hopes the danger will pass. Years or even decades later, reminders of the event can trigger this response, causing panic, fear, and anxiety. Understanding this physiological response plays a significant part in defining trauma and its enduring and often intrusive impacts.

In the end, defining trauma helps us grasp its complexities and broad-ranging effects, but it's not about boxing up experiences or categorizing people into groups. Understanding the nature of trauma is significant; however, each person's journey through trauma and healing is highly individual and deserves acknowledgment and respect.

As we venture further into the depths of trauma, there's a beacon of hope to bear in mind: Trauma may be part of your story, but it does not define you. You are more than the pain experienced, the struggles endured, and the feelings of despair. Grappling with the ghosts of traumatic pasts is a harrowing journey, but there's strength and resilience to be found in the very act of survival. And most encouraging of all, while trauma may leave a profound mark, it can be healed.

# Identifying Trauma in Your Life

In your journey of understanding trauma, identifying it in your own life is an important step. Maybe you've been struggling with unexplained emotions, distressed relationships, or lingering fears. But it's not always easy to pinpoint that these feelings or behaviors originate from trauma. Chances are, you could be grappling with trauma without even recognizing it.

Before we dive in, it's important to note that trauma doesn't always stem from a single, traumatic event.

Sometimes it's a culmination of several small incidents, termed 'complex trauma' by many experts. From the outside, they may seem insignificant, but they can leave a profound impact over time. There's no hierarchy in trauma — it doesn't discriminate based on the scale of the event. With this said, the first step is to break down the past and look at experiences that may have left a lasting mark.

You can begin by identifying any encounters with violence, bullying, physical or emotional abuse, abandonment, car accidents, or the death of a loved one. It's these overt traumas that first come to mind, and there's no escaping their significant impact. But besides such easily recognizable traumatic events, there's more subtle and insidious kinds of trauma that are often overlooked.

Neglect, for instance, can have detrimental effects on a child's psyche. Consistent dismissal of needs or feelings, humiliation, verbal degradation, or a caregiver's inability to express warmth all fall under emotional neglect. Similarly, enduring poverty, living in a high-crime neighborhood, parental substance misuse, or being part of a minority group in an oppressive society can all lead to chronic trauma.

Also, the vicarious trauma that results from witnessing the suffering of others should not be dismissed. First responders, healthcare professionals, or even individuals exposed to others' traumatic events through the media can experience this type of trauma.

It's possible to carry trauma without fully comprehending its weight. Sometimes, your body sends signals, expressing the pain inflicted on your psyche. Symptoms may present themselves emotionally, through feelings of hopelessness, chronic anxiety, depression, and emotional detachment. You may find it difficult to manage emotional responses, leading to frequent outbursts or withdrawal. Remember, these feelings are not a reflection of weakness but signs of unhealed wounds.

Physical symptoms can also be indicators of trauma. Unexplained fatigue, recurring nightmares, difficulty sleeping, and severe startle responses are few among many. You may also experience somatic symptoms, where psychological distress expresses itself through physical pain like chronic headaches or stomachaches.

Moreover, unhealthy coping mechanisms can also point towards unresolved trauma. These might include substance dependence, self-harm, disordered eating, or other forms of self-destructive behavior. Remember, these behaviors are not personal failings but desperate attempts to deal with an overwhelming pain.

But even with these signs, identifying trauma is not always clear-cut. You might have repressed traumatic memories in a bid to protect yourself, making them challenging to uncover. One possible sign of this repression is when you find patches of your memory to be grey or missing, especially from childhood.

If any of this resonates with you, it's essential to know that you're not alone. It's not unusual to disregard such experiences or their effects, mainly because acknowledging them can be painful. However, identifying the presence of trauma is the first step toward healing. It offers the chance to understand your experiences and reactions better and initiates the journey of reclamation.

Bringing light to past trauma is not about living in the past. Instead, it's about unpacking the baggage that weighs down on you. Unprocessed trauma can imprison you in subtle ways, and identifying it can often feel like discovering a key to a locked door.

In the next sections, we will explore how trauma, once identified, impacts your emotional and physical wellbeing. We will also journey through true stories of survivors, the strategies they used for healing, and ultimately, how to rebuild your life. Although this might seem overwhelming, remember: it's okay to take your time and approach this at your own pace. Little by little, step by step, you will move towards a more freeing and fulfilling life, one where past traumas no longer reside at the helm, but instead, become part of a powerful narrative of resilience and strength.

## How Inherited Family Trauma Shapes Who We Are and How to End the Cycle

Throughout our lives, we unwittingly carry the wounds of our ancestors, an invisible load sheepishly tucked into our emotional luggage. This subconscious legacy is a phenomenon known as inherited family trauma. It's a powerful, formative thread woven into the fabric of our identities, unbeknownst to most of us. The adversity and pain suffered by our forebears can subtly shape our behavior, attitudes, and responses to situations. Let's delve into how this can occur and more importantly, how we can break these often-destructive patterns.

Research has shown that trauma can be passed down through generations via epigenetic changes. Essentially, trauma can alter our DNA, the very building blocks of life, and this modified DNA can be passed on to our offspring. In this way, experiences of severe trauma may not just affect the individual who lived through it, but their descendants too.

While these revelations might appear daunting, they bring to light an essential perspective. If you've ever felt inexplicably anxious, plagued by unattributable fears, or conversely resistant to the experiences of your ancestors, the invisible hands of inherited family trauma may be at work.

But how does one go about breaking this cycle? Just as trauma can be inherited, so too, can healing. A crucial leap towards the healing process starts with identifying and acknowledging the inherited family trauma. It's only by unveiling the residual heartache hidden in our inherited stories that we can begin taking the necessary steps to heal.

Recognizing the symptoms of inherited trauma isn't always easy. Signs often surface as unexplained fears, persistent feelings of sadness, guilt, or shame, inexplicable panic and anxiety disorders, recurrent nightmares, or intrusive thoughts. The vagueness of these signs makes it even more imperative to explore one's lineage, to be curious about the emotional legacy handed down.

Building a comprehensive family history can bring any patterns of trauma into sharp relief, illuminating how these patterns can be echoing into your present. Begin by examining how your ancestors lived, their experiences, the challenges they faced, and any unresolved pain they might have suffered. By doing this, it can help draw the lineage between their life experiences and your psychological landscape.

Confronting the truths about past family trauma is dramatically healing – it's akin to turning on a light in a long-dark room. It will be challenging and emotionally taxing, but it's a crucial step for liberating oneself from the specter of inherited grief. Seek support during this process, as grappling with these revelations can stir up intense emotions.

A creative form of therapy like narrative therapy can be invaluable in this. By crafting a new narrative around the trauma, you can begin to distance yourself from it and the pain associated. It helps you perceive your family history and the inherent trauma less as a fixed blueprint of your destiny and more as an influence you have the power to reshape.

Mindfulness practice is another potent tool that can play an integral role in healing inherited family trauma. This process of cultivating acute awareness can help ground you in the present, detaching from the unsettling relics of the past. It's a gentle approach that nudges you to acknowledge your emotions without judgment, ultimately fostering resilience in the face of inherited traumas.

There are various healing modalities - holistic practices, energy healing, somatic therapies, and systematic constellations, among others - that may provide complementary support in resolving and overcoming inherited family trauma. Remember, there is no blanket solution for everyone - your healing journey is individual to you, directed towards the ultimate goal of breaking the cycle of inherited trauma.

Transcending the powerful grip of inherited family trauma might feel like a monumental task, but it's a journey well worth taking. It's about giving yourself permission to draw a firm line between the past and present, asserting your mental and emotional boundaries.

It's important to remember that putting an end to this cyclical trauma doesn't mean erasing your past or your family's history. It's about acknowledging pain, embracing healing, and understanding that while your ancestors' experiences have shaped you, they don't have to define you.

Breaking the chain of inherited trauma is the greatest gift you can offer future generations. And while this journey of healing and transformation will pose several challenges, remember, every step you take towards releasing the bondage of your ancestral past paves the way for a healthier, happier and liberated future—for you and for generations to come.

As you navigate this path of exploration, healing, and liberation, keep in mind that you aren't alone. There's a collective of individuals worldwide experiencing, enduring, and rising above inherited family trauma. We are all, in our ways and times, distilling our stories from pain to one of triumph over inherited trauma.

By confronting and addressing the trauma in your lineage, you're paving the path towards healing and hope, shifting from a lineage of trauma to a legacy of resilience, strength, and liberation.

## Common Misconceptions About Trauma

As we delve deeper into understanding trauma, it's crucial to address and dispel the common misconceptions surrounding this critical matter. These misconceptions, if left unchecked, can stall or even obstruct the healing process, prolong the sufferer's struggle, and delay their reclaiming of a fuller life. Hence, gaining clear perspective and throwing light on these oft-held fallacies is a fundamental step towards healing.

The first misconception is that trauma is an immediate result of a single catastrophic event. While it's true that acute traumatizing events like natural disasters, violent crimes, or severe accidents can indeed precipitate trauma, trauma can also accrue over prolonged periods of repeated, severe stress. This will be known as complex trauma or chronic trauma.

The trauma from chronic emotional abuse, neglect, poverty, discrimination, or other forms of psychological harm can be as damaging if not more damaging than acute shocks. Hence, it's vital to understand that trauma isn't always an overnight occurrence; it can build up over time.

The second common misunderstanding is that trauma is a sign of weakness or lack of toughness in a person. Nothing could be further from the truth. Everyone's response to stress or danger is inherently individual, and the occurrence of trauma isn't indicative of weakness or insufficiency. It speaks more about the overwhelming nature of the experiential stressors rather than the person's character or personal toughness.

A related myth is that only those with mental health issues are predisposed to experience trauma. This flawed belief propagates the notion that trauma isn't a widespread human problem but rather confined to a select few with specific mental health issues. Again, this is misleading.

Any person, regardless of the state of their mental health, can be traumatized given sufficiently intense or chronic stress or danger. It's vital to normalize trauma as a universal issue that can potentially affect anyone, rather than stigmatizing it as a problem limited to those with mental health conditions.

Another misunderstanding regarding trauma is the idea that time alone will heal all wounds. Yes, time is a significant element in healing, but it's not the panacea for trauma. Without proactive steps such as seeking professional help, adopting self-help techniques, or help from a supportive community, the wounds of trauma may fester, becoming even more profound and debilitating.

The idea that traumas are meant to be forgotten and that discussing them is too painful is yet another misconception. While revisiting traumatic events can indeed be painful, sheathing them in silence might only perpetuate the trauma. Professionally guided conversation and therapeutic techniques can help individuals safely explore and process their traumatic experiences, leading towards genuine healing.

One more fallacy is the belief that trauma cannot be inherited. Though it may sound implausible, research now suggests that trauma can indeed be handed down through generations in specific ways, affecting us on both psychological and physiological levels. Understanding this can provide profound insights into our inherent susceptibilities and unresolved emotional baggage.

Lastly, there's a misconception that once traumatized, a person will remain so forever. This is not the case. While trauma indeed leaves a lasting mark, being traumatized isn't a permanent status. With effective methods of therapy, appropriate assistance, and self-improvement practices, individuals can rise above their condition and experience renewed purpose, peace, and zest for life.

It's vital to recognize these misleading beliefs for what they are, fallacies that prevent us from understanding the true nature of trauma and its healing process. Grasping the complexity and intricacies of trauma can help us empathize better with those struggling and also equip us effectively in our own personal battles to regain control over our lives after trauma.

Remember, knowledge is power: debunking these misconceptions about trauma isn't just part of educating ourselves. It's a crucial first step on the path of healing and reclamation after trauma. Understanding the true nature of our adversaries, in this case, unfounded beliefs, empowers us to devise an effective plan of action to combat them.

As we look forward to subsequent chapters, we will uncover the manifold impacts of trauma, both physically and emotionally. We will shine a light on the survivors' stories, who have walked the path of healing and emerged victoriously. We will explore proven healing strategies, ones that have been transformative in liberating individuals from the clutches of trauma.

Let this debunking of falsities about trauma today fuel a better understanding, and arm you with the right perspective which is absolutely vital in reclaiming your life. With truth, love, and courage, you can conquer trauma, and authentically embrace the wholeness of life amidst its inevitable trials.

# Chapter 2: The Impact of Trauma

After we've explored the nature of trauma, it's time to delve into the profound ways in which it affects our lives. The ripple effects of trauma, like a stone thrown into a still pond, exist in waves of emotional and physical symptoms that can impact our overall wellbeing, sometimes for a lifetime. The emotional fallout from traumatic experiences can manifest in countless shapes and forms, ranging from anger, guilt and self-blame, to depression, anxiety, and even ripples into PTSD - a shell of constant unrest that one carries around silently. But it doesn't end there, these emotional repercussions intertwine with our bodies, and seep into our physical health. Mysterious physiological issues, unexplainable aches, and even chronic illnesses can be ignited, powered by the fuel of unresolved trauma. However, the realities of trauma's reign don't end with these palpable symptoms. We're dealing with a long-term toll, a silent strain that persists, often unseen, unaccounted for, and unrecognized. Trauma, more rampant than ever, remains a silent epidemic, brushed under the carpet of our collective consciousness.

Never underestimate the power that trauma wields over individuals, it's more than the initial shock, it's a wave of entrapping patterns that can debilitate and hollow out the brightest of lives. But we're here, together, to shed light on the shadows cast by trauma, spark conversations, fuel understanding, and ultimately, start the turning of the tides.

# Emotional Consequences of Trauma

Trauma finds a way to touch every aspect of our lives, no matter how much we try to keep it at bay. While physical damages may be apparent immediately, the emotional consequences of trauma often simmer underneath, slowly eating away at our peace, happiness, and overall well-being. Recognizing these emotional effects and acknowledging them is the first step towards healing.

Following a traumatic experience, it's routine to feel intense, sometimes overwhelming emotions. These include feelings of panic, fear, and unpredictability. The world you've always known suddenly becomes a source of danger and the unknown. This fear often morphs into anxiety, leading to restlessness, constant worry, and the inability to focus.

Depression is another common outcome of trauma. Plunged into a deep abyss of sadness, survivors gradually lose interest in previously enjoyed activities, face changes in appetite, and can have difficulties in sleeping. They might also struggle with feelings of guilt, worthlessness, and underperformance.

Among the emotional consequences of trauma, anger is a frequent visitor. Some people may direct this anger outwards, towards others, leading to conflicts and strained relationships. Others may turn this anger inward, resulting in guilt, self-blame, and self-loathing. And when this anger becomes chronic, it can bring about serious physical health complications.

Many trauma survivors grapple with a sense of shame, often linked to self-blame. They internalize the trauma, attributing it to their actions or inactions, and believe they could have somehow prevented it. This shame can make them feel jammed in their healing journey, crippled by silence, isolation, and self-judgment.

The shock of a traumatic event sometimes provokes a detachment from reality, leading to disassociation. This can manifest itself as 'spacing out', forgetting about parts or the entirety of the traumatic event, or having a feeling of seeing the event play out rather than participating in it. While this is a coping mechanism for some, it can be quite distressing and disruptive over time.

Trust becomes a significant casualty of trauma. A reluctance to trust people, the surroundings, and even oneself, emerges, making relationships complicated and causing survivors to feel lonely and isolated. This loss of trust is frequently linked to feelings of vulnerability and powerlessness.

Survivors of trauma often struggle with intrusive thoughts and memories related to the traumatic experience. These flashbacks can be triggered by anything remotely connected to the trauma, leading to distress, anxiety, and panic attacks. They can be so vivid that the person feels they're reliving the trauma, jolting their sense of reality.

Emotional blunting - the inability to feel pleasure or pain - is another common symptom seen in trauma survivors. It's as if the person has erected an emotional wall around themselves to prevent any feelings from getting in. It creates an emotional numbness, leading to a sense of isolation and disconnection from others.

The emotional turmoil can also induce sleep disturbances, be it insomnia or nightmares. Sleep becomes riddled with anxiety, making relaxation and rest an uphill task. This sleep deprivation can further augment feelings of irritation, fatigue, and difficulty in concentration, ensuring a vicious cycle.

Despite these various emotional consequences of trauma, remember that the human spirit is remarkably resilient. These impacts don't define you or your life. You're not broken or weak. Rather, you're shaped in extraordinary ways by the experiences that you've lived through.

Recognizing and understanding these emotional effects of trauma exhibits your strength and proves that you're already on the path towards healing. Each sign is your mind's way of trying to process and make sense of what happened, and they are calls for attention, care, and gentle understanding. It's okay to not feel okay. It's okay to need help. It's okay to ask for help.

As we delve deeper into this journey, you'll discover the tools and resources to navigate through these emotions, to tame the storm inside you, and to heal and rewire your brain. Your trauma does matter. Your feelings do count. But remember, your trauma is something you experienced; it is not who you are. You're far more than the pain and hurt you've endured.

You, a survivor of trauma, can retake control over your life and your emotions. Through understanding, patience, affirmative action, and compassionate self-care, you can mend the emotional scars left by trauma and restore balance in your life. Know that the emotional aftermath of trauma is complex, but so are you, in incredibly resilient and brilliant ways.

Bear in mind, healing from trauma is not about forgetting or erasing the past. You can't change what happened, but you can change how it affects you. Embrace the journey towards healing, acknowledge your feelings, trust the process, and remember - healing is not linear. You're allowed to have setbacks. With each step taken, you're rewriting your story - from one of pain and trauma to one of strength, hope, and triumph.

## Physical Symptoms of Trauma

The impact of trauma on an individual's life is multi-dimensional, affecting not only the emotional and psychological fragments, but also the physical self. The body, in fact, keeps a keen and immediate record of the trauma endured, often reacting instinctively to the circumstances with its unique physical signs and symptoms.

One of the more overt physical signs of trauma can be changes in sleeping patterns. Some individuals may find themselves sleeping too much, while others might struggle with insomnia or erratic sleep patterns. Difficulty in falling asleep or maintaining sleep might manifest, often accompanied by nightmares or flashbacks related to the traumatic episode.

Extreme fatigue is another common physical symptom could arise from trauma. As the emotional and mental strain endeavor to deal with the traumatic event, the physical body often reflects this exertion through an overwhelming feeling of tiredness and lack of energy.

In line with fatigue, there can be a significant strain on the immune system. As the body goes into a state of heightened alert following a traumatic event, resources are shifted towards managing the stress response. This can lead to general vulnerabilities in the body such as getting sick more easily, slower healing, and increased aches and pains.

The human body has a particularly sensitive gastrointestinal system, which can be greatly affected by trauma. Symptoms such as altered appetite, constipation, diarrhea, or stomach aches are not uncommon in individuals dealing with trauma. For some, these can manifest as an eating disorder, exacerbated further when the trauma is related to body image or self-perception.

Certain physical conditions like chronic pain and somatic symptoms may also be linked to trauma. Somatic symptoms are physical ailments without a direct physiological reason, mainly driven by psychological stressors. For instance, people might experience inexplicable headaches, backaches, or other types of physical discomfort.

Rapid heartbeats, palpitations or difficulty in breathing are also indicative physical stress markers. Many trauma victims experience what feels like mini panic attacks, where they can't catch their breath or their heart seems to be pounding out of their chest. It's the body's way of signaling that it's still locked in a fight-or-flight survival mode.

For some people, trauma can lead to significant weight changes. This could be a result of overeating or undereating, using food as a coping mechanism or refusing to eat as a form of self-punishment.

Being hypersensitive to sounds, lights, or even touch is another after-effect of trauma on the physical self. The body continually perceives danger even when the actual threat has passed, leading to heightened senses.

Interestingly, an individual's posture and movement could also reveal trauma histories. If you notice someone continually guarded or flinching easily at sudden movements, it could hint at past trauma.

Trauma sufferers may also experience psychomotor agitation, characterized by repetitive or restlessness movements. This might include pacing, wringing hands, uncontrolled leg movements or other similar physical responses.

Observe changes in sexual behavior too, as trauma, especially when it's sexual in nature, can result in a loss of interest in sexual activity, dysfunctions or alternatively an increase in risky sexual behaviors.

To sum up, these physical symptoms serve as the physical voice to internal emotional pain and mental turmoil. In their own quiet, yet profound ways, these signs act as alarm bells, indicating that an individual has gone through something traumatic and is trying hard to cope.

Identifying these physical symptoms is the first step to understanding how your body is responding to trauma. It's important to listen to these signals and seek help when needed. Remember, these physical manifestations are your body's way of expressing its need for healing.

In some ways, they form a silent reminder that it's time to help yourself recover from the trauma, to make pain a part of your strength, and to plant seeds of hope in the desert of your desolation. You are more than your trauma, and your journey towards healing can begin today.

## The Long-Term Toll of Trauma

Trauma can manifest in many ways. The impact is not always immediate or apparent, but it often leaves long-lasting scars. Unaddressed, it can change your life, creating ripples of consequence that extend well into the future.

Emotionally, trauma can lead to a whole spectrum of issues, both apparent and concealed. It's not uncommon for survivors to grapple with a wide array of mental health disorders like Post-Traumatic Stress Disorder (PTSD), depression or anxiety. These conditions can persist for years, sometimes surfacing long after the traumatizing event itself.

People who go through trauma often experience profound changes in their mood and personality. They might find themselves becoming prone to anger, or unusually withdrawn. Sometimes, they may struggle to feel anything at all, as feelings of emotional numbness take hold. This emotional toll can drastically impact their relationships, both personal and professional, creating a secondary layer of difficulty to manage.

Trauma can compromise cognitive function as well. One might find it hard to concentrate, or struggle with decision-making. In more severe cases, they might suffer from memory problems or confusion, hindering their ability to function in their daily life.

Physically, trauma can also leave its mark. Insomnia or nightmares are common problems, while others may experience chronic fatigue. Some survivors might find themselves facing inexplicable aches and pains, or startling changes in eating habits which can lead to significant weight loss or gain. These can often be physical manifestations of the emotional and cognitive disturbances they are experiencing.

Consequently, the long-term health implications of such trauma-related symptoms can't be ignored. Persistent stress and anxiety can compromise the immune system, leaving survivors more vulnerable to illness. Plus, disruptions in eating and sleeping can further destabilize health, while chronic pain can actually lead to metabolic changes which heighten the risk of various diseases.

Survivors who resort to substance abuse, as a means to cope, expose themselves to numerous health risks as well. This self-medication, unfortunately, serves only to compound the issue further, creating a vicious cycle that leaves the survivor trapped in constant suffering.

Yet what is perhaps even more dire than these tangible effects is the change in perception trauma can inflict. Many survivors begin to view themselves differently, their self-esteem battered by their experiences. They may see themselves as weak, broken, or as damaged goods, causing an erosion of their self-image that's difficult to repair.

This altered self-perception can serve to perpetuate feelings of worthlessness and hopelessness, further exacerbating depression and anxiety. It can also lead to self-isolation, as survivors, convinced of their own unworthiness, retreat from human connection. This lack of social support, in turn, can make the healing process even more daunting.

The effects of trauma can also extend to spiritual and existential beliefs. Survivors may find their faith shaken, their understanding of the world and their place within it severely affronted. This spiritual toll can leave them grappling with profound questions about justice, fairness, and humanity.

It cannot be understated how significantly the long-term impacts of trauma can affect a survivor's quality of life. Yet, as debilitating as these effects may be, it's important to remember that they don't define who you are. They don't control you, and they don't need to dictate your future.

Acknowledging the profound effect trauma can have is the first step toward reclaiming your power. Understanding its impacts allows you to better comprehend your experiences and begin the journey of healing. Just as traumas are varied and diverse, so too are the possibilities for recovery. Resilience is possible, and with it, you can reclaim your life.

You don't need to navigate this journey alone. Reaching out to others, be they trusted friends or professionals, can lift you. You can seek solace and support in shared experiences and empathy. Trauma may shape us, but we are not victims. We are survivors, and we can rise.

Remember, healing is not linear. There will be setbacks, but there will also be victories. Every small step you take towards reclaiming your life from trauma is a triumph. This long-term battle is tough, but within you resides an irrefutable strength and resilience. You've endured the trauma; now it's time to take back control and walk firmly on the path of healing.

## The Invisible Epidemic

Trauma is often called an "invisible epidemic," a scourge that goes largely unseen but carries with it deep, lasting impacts. Yet, its invisibility can be deceiving; it's far more prevalent than most people realize. It lurks beneath the surface, quietly shaping lives and dictating actions. The invisibility of trauma also adds to its enigma, making it harder for those affected to identify and confront it.

The 'invisible' nature of trauma extends to its impacts as well. To the external observer, symptoms might be interpreted as personality traits or character quirks rather than signs of trauma. A person living with unresolved trauma may be seen as introverted, overly emotional, or unpredictable rather than as someone struggling to cope with the impacts of traumatic experiences. This lack of understanding compounds the pain of experiencing trauma and can result in struggles going unrecognized and untreated.

Unfortunately, the invisibility of trauma also masks its widespread prevalence. An unseen epidemic, trauma cuts across socioeconomic lines, ethnicities and backgrounds, making no exceptions. Signs of traumatic distress might resonate in the boardroom as much as in the schoolroom, and it impacts both those living in well-kept homes in peaceful neighborhoods and those subjected to violence and poverty.

Individuals impacted by trauma might express its effects through physical symptoms, such as unexplained pain, chronic illnesses, or sleep disturbances. They may display behavior changes, such as irritability, emotional outbursts, or substance abuse—symptoms often misattributed to other factors. As a result, these individuals might not even realize that they're battling the invisible onslaught of trauma.

That's one of the insidious aspects of trauma: its ability to quietly intrude upon many facets of the human experience. It can shape emotional responses, influence relationships, skew perspectives of the self, and disturb mental and physical health, yet often goes undetected or dismissed as simply 'just the way things are'.

The very invisibility of trauma makes it all the more critical to understand, identify, and address it. Much like a physical disease, early detection and intervention can significantly affect the healing process. And the first step towards healing is acknowledging the trauma embedded in one's life history and its lingering impacts.

Seeing the unseen involves building an understanding of oneself and the patterns we incorporate into our lives. By recognizing patterns of behavior, emotional responses, and physical symptoms that may be linked to prior traumatic experiences, we can begin to make sense of that which previously seemed inexplicable.

But how exactly do you recognize these patterns when trauma operates beneath the surface? Start by paying attention to emotional reactions, bodily responses, patterns of thought, and interpersonal dynamics. By being attentive to subtle cues we usually overlook, we empower ourselves to confront the 'invisible epidemic.'

Next, remember that trauma can emerge from experiences not typically labeled traumatic. Divorce, job loss, relocation, or illness—these can all potentially cause trauma. While these experiences might seem ordinary and unavoidable parts of life, when their impacts seep into our daily functioning in disruptive ways, they may well be sources of trauma.

Spreading awareness about trauma—its symptoms, impacts, and healing pathways—is a crucial step to address the invisible epidemic. We can foster a society that better understands trauma, its penetrating reach, and the pivotal importance of addressing it. By bringing trauma out from the shadows, we allow those affected to recognize their adversities, seek help, and begin their journey towards healing.

Ultimately, the journey to healing from trauma involves recognizing its presence, understanding its effects, and committing to the healing process. With the right resources, compassion, and perseverance, anyone grappling with the invisible epidemic can reclaim control over their life and move towards a brighter, more fulfilled future.

Remember: Trauma may be an epidemic, but it needn't define you. By acknowledging its invisibility, we shine a light on an otherwise unseen phenomenon, empowering individuals to confront their traumatic pasts and carve a path towards healing. In this way, we seek to convert a hushed plight into a rallying cry for resilience, recovery, and renewal.

In the following chapters, we'll explore real-life stories of survivors who have navigated their way through the invisible epidemic and have come out stronger on the other side. We'll also delve into strategies, techniques, and resources that can assist individuals on their journey towards healing from trauma.

# Chapter 3: True Life Stories of Survivors

Delving into the heart of our subject matter, this chapter presents the raw, unfiltered accounts of individuals who have battled and triumphed over trauma. Each narrative is unique and poignant, speaking volumes of the human spirit's resilience in the face of adversity. 'Rhonda's Reclamation,' for example, takes us through a harrowing tale of abuse, and a subsequent reclaiming of personal strength and identity. 'Jake's Journey' addresses trauma inflicted by societal neglect and peer rejection, revealing to us a side of trauma often hidden from the public eye, while 'Clara Conquers' shows us how it's possible to turn pain inflicted by intimate partner violence into a force for positive change. Together, these narratives unveil the many faces of trauma and recovery, offering comfort, inspiration, and insights about the healing process. As we journey with them, we glean nuggets of wisdom tailored from first-hand experiences that make all the difference in battling trauma. Learn from their steps and missteps, their triumphs, and most importantly, their refusal to be defined by their pasts. We'll also delve into various conversations on trauma, resilience, and healing – drawing lessons from survivors across diverse backgrounds.

## Survivor Story: Rhonda's Reclamation

The air was thick and heavy, much like Rhonda's heart, the first time she stepped foot into her therapist's office. A lifelong struggle with anxiety and depression, fueled by a past marred by trauma, had led her to this moment. The journey had not been easy, a constant rollercoaster through stormy seas of tumultuous emotions. Yet, she was there, a testament to her quiet but formidable resilience.

As a young woman, Rhonda had endured the unendurable, a brutal attack that shattered her confidence and left deep emotional scars. A shroud of fear, vulnerability, and self-doubt had enveloped her life, making each day a challenge to navigate.

Initially, Rhonda felt trapped in her trauma, defined by the pain and the shame associated with it. Most therapy sessions were a blur of tears, silent sobs-screams of a pain, too intense for words. She bore her anguish with grace, ever willing to uncover and confront the patches of her past that hurt the most.

Through the process of one-on-one therapy, Rhonda learned to acknowledge her trauma and its devastating effects on her life. It was not about forgetting the horror but about reducing its stranglehold on her life. Her gifted therapist used elements of Cognitive Behavioral Therapy, replacing destructive mindsets with healthier coping mechanisms and beliefs.

Journaling played a pivotal role in Rhonda's reclamation journey. At first, the pages were filled with raw pain and hopelessness, reflections of the agony within her. However, over time, the narrative evolved, showcasing Rhonda's resilience, her growing strength, and her indomitable will to heal.

Furthermore, Rhonda explored healing through mindfulness, taught to stay present, to not allow the echo of the past to seep into the now. It was tough, but the more she tried, the more she learned to separate the past from the present, steadily regaining control of her mental landscape.

Colonizing her life once marred by trauma were newfound friendships, echoing empathy and understanding. She realized that isolation had been a corrosive element in her healing journey. Building connections with others who had experienced trauma enabled her to feel seen, heard, and validated.

However, healing is not a linear path, and Rhonda's journey was not devoid of stumbling blocks. Days of setback were awash with frustration and a crippling fear of never truly healing. Yet, within those moments of despair, there was a quiet defiance, a growing reassurance that she could, and she would, overcome.

By refusing to allow her trauma to define her, Rhonda transformed it into her greatest source of power. It was in her own willingness to confront and dismantle the seemingly unshakable shackles of her past, where she discovered an inner strength, an unyielding spirit that no hardship could ever extinguish.

Through her passages of pain, Rhonda recognized that she was not merely a survivor, but a warrior. Her trauma was a part of her history, but it did not and could not outline her future. It had indeed shaped her, but she was the sculptor, chiselling away the fear, carving out courage, and revealing an inner magnificence that had always been there.

Today, Rhonda is not just living, she is thriving— a vibrant testament to her resilience. She has cultivated a thriving professional life and continues to build meaningful relationships. Through it all, self-care and gratitude have become cornerstones of her life.

Rhonda's reclamation of her life following trauma is a testament that healing is possible. It's a long journey, undeniably tumultuous, but one that reveals strength and resilience within oneself. Her story carries a powerful message of hope; a beacon for those who may be at the start of their healing journeys.

It's crucial to remember that, much like Rhonda, you too have the capacity to heal, to reclaim your life from the grips of trauma. You are stronger than you think, and with the right tools, help, and mindset, you can chart your own path of healing.

Rhonda's story is one of hope, resilience, empowerment, and strength. A tale of a soul rising from the shadows of trauma, into the glorious light of self-love and empowerment. Her journey is but one of many, stirring the will within us to reclaim our lives in the face of trauma, to not just survive, but to thrive.

## Survivor Story: Jake's Journey

Jake's journey through trauma is one that began in an ordinary small town in the midwest. When he was just eight years old, his peaceful existence was shattered by a devastating house fire that claimed the lives of both his parents, instantly plunging him into a world of grief and helplessness.

In the months following the tragedy, Jake found himself tossed from one relative's home to another. The constant changes were disorienting, and further compounded his trauma. During this period, he exhibited signs of Post-Traumatic Stress Disorder (PTSD) - suffering from frequent nightmares, abnormally heightened startle responses, and a tendency to isolate himself.

Recognizing that Jake was in desperate need of help, his aunt Laura, the last among the relatives with whom Jake was shuffled, sought professional assistance. It was through the compassionate and skilled intervention of a trauma-focused therapist that Jake slowly began his journey towards recovery.

His practitioner used Cognitive Behavior Therapy (CBT), allowing Jake to understand and reframe his distorted thoughts and beliefs. This technique was instrumental in helping him overcome feelings of guilt and self-blame that he had harbored as a direct result of the traumatic event. He was taught that the loss of his parents was due to unpredictable circumstances beyond his control, tearing down the misguided notion that he could have somehow prevented their deaths.

Jake was also introduced to the method of Eye Movement Desensitization and Reprocessing (EMDR). EMDR was a challenging, yet transformative step in his therapy. As he revisited his traumatic memories within a safe and controlled environment, he found himself gradually able to decrease his emotional distress and develop more adaptive beliefs.

Jake was determined to support his formal therapy with personal self-help techniques. Mindfulness practices became a crucial part of his daily routine. He learned to focus his mind on the present, recognizing and accepting his feelings without judgement. This helped him cultivate resilience and a greater sense of control over his thoughts and feelings.

In addition to mindfulness, Jake also embraced the technique of trauma recovery through journaling. He found that the act of pouring his thoughts onto paper allowed for a tangible vent of emotions. Moreover, he noticed that, with time, retracing his feelings in previous entries initiated a marked shift in perspective, providing a glimpse of his personal growth and healing progression.

Over the span of several years, Jake began to regain a semblance of normalcy and control over his life. As he processed his trauma, he learned to develop trust in himself and others. Gradually, he managed to foster healthy and supportive relationships and was, through hard work and great perseverance, able to reintegrate into professional life successfully.

There were always setbacks along the way, of course. The road to healing from such profound trauma is never straight and smooth. But with every hurdle encountered, Jake continued to push forward with grit and determination, drawing strength from the progress he had made.

The journey was not an easy one, and it continues to this day. However, Jake's resilience serves as a source of inspiration for many other trauma survivors. Through the power of healing strategies, self-help techniques, immense resilience, and ongoing support, Jake has been able to reclaim his life after trauma, a testament to the human ability to survive and thrive in the face of adversity.

The objective of sharing Jake's journey is not to provide a standard trajectory of trauma recovery - because everyone's path towards healing is unique. But rather, Jake's story is meant to serve as a beacon of hope, a testament to the fact that no matter the extent of trauma one has experienced, with patience, effort, and appropriate support, healing is attainable.

Remember, the impact of trauma can be deeply ingrained, but you are not defeated by these experiences. Just like Jake, you too have the potential to go beyond surviving and move towards thriving, reclaiming your life after trauma.

Jake's journey should remind us that in order to overcome trauma, it's not just about reaching the final destination, but growing stronger with each step forward. The human spirit is resilient, and with the right tools and determination, each of us can find our way out of even the deepest trenches of despair.

# Survivor Story: Clara Conquers

In the delicate fabric of interpersonal relationships and personal fragility, Clara's story emerges as an inspiring testament of resilience, healing, and triumph over trauma. Raised as an only child in unstable circumstances, Clara's life was marred early on with the harsh realities of domestic violence and emotional neglect.

Her parents, both victims of their own unattended trauma, inflicted their pain and hardships onto Clara. A lonely and chaotic childhood could've easily predisposed her to a life led by fear, anxiety, and constant self-doubt. Yet, her story unfolds like a beacon of hope, a testament to the human spirit's resilience and an exemplification of triumph over widespread adversity. She paints a vivid picture of coping mechanisms and healing strategies that have paved her path to recovery.

Early in her journey through chaos, Clara realized the power of self-reliance. In a world where her immediate guardians were supposed to offer protection yet were the cause of her torment, her survival instincts grew strong. She developed an uncanny ability to detach herself emotionally, a defense mechanism that allowed her to escape her harsh reality temporarily.

However, once she left her turbulent home to attend a University in a distant city, the feelings she'd suppressed and tactics she'd used to cope began to surface in unexpected ways. Now free from her immediate tormentors, Clara was still haunted by the ghost of her neglected past.

Inspired by some psychology courses in college, she understood the idea of trauma and its consequences—not just immediate, but also long-term. Looking at her reflexive defenses, her constant state of hypervigilance, and the struggles in forming and maintaining healthy relationships, Clara realized she needed to channel her will to survive into a desire to truly live.

Clara started her healing journey with self-reflection, creating an internal dialogue about her experiences. This marked the beginning of a challenging, soul-stirring voyage. She began journaling as a way to make sense of her experiences, starting a dialogue with the child within her who was still terrified, confused, and hurt.

Though difficult initially, Clara slowly started to make entries about her childhood—reliving the painful memories, but this time as a detached observer. In the process, she made a critical discovery: the power of narrative. She learned that, looking back at her past through a different lens, she could start reshaping her perspective.

Her next step was acknowledging the magnitude of her experiences and giving herself the permission to feel the pain she had systematically suppressed. This entailed opening the floodgates to a torrent of emotions. But resolving to stay the course, Clara continued with her self-reflection, assimilation, and emotional expression through journaling.

This processing of emotions and experiences was exhausting yet cathartic. Clara also sought professional help in therapy and began practicing mindfulness. She realized that it was not just about healing old wounds, but also about learning fresh patterns of living.

Through counseling and therapy, Clara recognized her inherent worth. With cognitive behavioural therapy, she was able to challenge her destructive thought patterns and replace them with positive affirmations. Gradually, she rebuilt her shattered self-esteem, learned to respect the person she had become, and embarked on maintaining healthier relationships.

Clara's story brims with lessons of audacious survivorship and reflects the power of resilience and determination. Moreover, it highlights the importance of understanding trauma, seeking help, and actively investing in self-healing.

One of the most enlightening revelations from Clara's experience is the importance of forgiveness—not necessarily for those who caused the harm, but for oneself. She realized that in forgiving herself for not fighting back, for not knowing better, she was finally able to liberate herself from the chains of her past.

Most importantly, Clara's story serves as a cautionary tale that trauma can't be bypassed. But with courage, self-awareness, and desire for healing, one can move from surviving to thriving. Today, Clara stands tall, undefeated, a beacon of hope for others wading through the troubled waters of their traumatic past.

To paraphrase a statement Clara often uses: 'When life throws you into the brisk, tumultuous ocean of trauma, remember you have the strength to stay afloat and eventually, towards the shore.' This is Clara's triumph: meeting her challenges, and eventually conquering them on her path to recovery and self-discovery.

Clara's journey thus highlights what we often forget — everyone has the capacity to heal, the potential to evolve, and the right to thrive. Her narrative is a remarkable testament to the human spirit's resilience in the face of adversity and the sheer power of determination and hope.

## Conversations on Trauma, Resilience, and Healing

In the face of trauma, there's power in conversation, strength in shared stories and immense healing when words are woven together to convey the journeys of survivors. These are conversations about resilience and recovery, touching on dark moments, but more importantly, they spotlight how individuals emerged from these shadows, stronger and more enlightened.

One such conversation is with Michael, who endured years of traumatic experiences. Like many, he didn't understand trauma's depth and breadth initially, often dismissing the unsettling emotions. It was in acknowledging these feelings and sharing his experiences that Michael found the first steps towards healing.

The acknowledgement of Michael's trauma brought him face-to-face with his pain. The resilience and courage displayed are testaments to his ability to endure and overcome. The journey wasn't easy, nor linear, but through persistence and dedication, he found the tools necessary for the excavation of his healing path.

Kathleen's narrative significantly stands out as well. A survivor of domestic abuse, her trauma was intensely personal and complex. Her resilience story testifies to the constructive power of confronting your past. As she reconciled with these hard truths, it allowed her to disentangle herself from the patterns of victimhood.

For both Kathy and Michael, resilience wasn't just about enduring. It was about adapting and redefining themselves in the face of their traumatic experiences. They both found strength within, nurtured it, and that internal power has allowed them to ensure and push forward.

Healing doesn't mean forgetting or blocking out the trauma. It's more about holding space for that pain, recognizing the changes it brought, and using those changes to propel personal growth and transformation. Resiliency, in many ways, is a byproduct of this healing, born from accepting, navigating, and learning from pain instead of merely trying to erase it.

Eleanor's journey is another inspiring tale of healing. Following a car accident that nearly claimed her life, she grappled with physical and emotional trauma. She learned, over time, that healing often requires a holistic approach involving body, mind, and spirit.

The conversations with these survivors highlight common threads - the importance of acknowledging trauma, fostering resilience, and the power inherent in sharing personal narratives. They showcase that healing is not a solitary task but a shared responsibility that weaves in the experiences of others to create a collective strength.

From these compelling stories, it is clear that healing looks different for everyone. Some find solace in therapy, others in mindfulness practices or journaling. Some may find relief in medications, while others might prefer a more spiritual approach. The path to healing isn't identical for each person; it's a path tangled with personal and unique obstacles and triumphs.

These survivor conversations provide a stark reminder that while trauma can shatter us temporarily, resilience is the glue that reconstructs us. It's not about going back to the person you were before the trauma; it's about growing and evolving through the healing process.

These discussions also underscore that trauma survivors aren't alone in their struggle. There's a wider community filled with individuals who have walked similar paths, and their stories weave a supportive tapestry that victim can draw comfort, strength and inspiration from. Indeed, in conversations dwells connection – a force powerful enough to rupture the walls of loneliness which trauma often builds.

Let these narratives of resilience and healing be a testament to the indomitable human spirit. Embrace them not as a roadmap, but as touchstones reminding you of the power, strength, and courage present within you, waiting to propel you into a brighter, healthier future.

In sum, conversations on trauma, resilience, and healing, are a crucial element of the survivor's journey. They create a space to share, reflect, and learn – where experiences, both devastating and enlightening, become lessons. And most importantly, they become foundations upon which resilient towers rise – towers that overlook not devastation, but a landscape of untapped possibilities painted with hope.

So let's keep the conversations going. Let's keep listening, sharing, and healing; transforming our collective narrative from one of survival to one of thriving. The road to recovery might be challenging, but it's through stories of triumph over trauma that we find the courage and perseverance to face these challenges and emerge victorious.

# Chapter 4: Proven Strategies for Healing

Coming to terms with trauma is arduous, but understanding is half the battle. After shining a light on the many facets of trauma and hearing the inspiring stories of survival, we now delve into the crucial stage of healing. One of the foremost avenues to explore is the healing power our brain, mind, and body hold in trauma recovery. Simultaneously, overcoming trauma takes more than inner resolve. Formal therapy techniques such as Cognitive Behavior Therapy (CBT) and Eye Movement Desensitization and Reprocessing (EMDR) work wonders to reframe traumatic experiences and aid recovery. Alongside professional help, employing simple self-help techniques can provide extra support in your healing journey. Mindfulness becomes a powerful tool in calming the mind, while journaling can offer therapeutic release through transferring internal turmoil on paper. Scriptural meditation also serves as a potent remedy, offering solace and guidance through tough times. This combination of strategies outlines a diverse, yet comprehensive approach to healing from trauma, providing not only the stepping stones but also the ardent spirit to reach for the light at the end of the tunnel.

## Brain, Mind, and Body in the Healing of Trauma

The workings of the brain, mind, and body in the healing of trauma provide fascinating insights into the human capacity for resilience and recovery. Each plays a pivotal role in determining how we respond to traumatic events, as well as how we can navigate the journey towards healing. Understanding the integration between these aspects is not just scientific—it forms the foundation of holistic healing approaches, recognizing that to fully heal from trauma, we must address all elements of our being.

Firstly, it's crucial to understand the brain's role in dealing with trauma. When we face a traumatic event, our brain tries to protect us with its built-in survival mechanism—essentially, fight, flight, or freeze response. But sometimes, the trauma is so severe that the brain can't process it properly. As a result, traumatic memories might get stuck, not adequately stored or processed, leading to post-traumatic stress disorder (PTSD) or other trauma-related disorders.

Healing, therefore, involves re-engaging the brain in a safe environment to properly process these "stuck" memories. Techniques like neurofeedback and brain stimulation therapies have been proven particularly beneficial in helping the brain reprocess traumatic experiences. These methods aim to regulate the brain's activity, promoting its ability to cope with emotional stress and destabilizing thoughts.

Moving on to the mind, we must consider the psychological perspective of healing from trauma. Cognitive restructuring plays a crucial part in this process, as we learn to identify and challenge destructive thought patterns that keep us anchored to our trauma. Our belief system influences our perception of ourselves, our trauma, and our ability to recover. As such, it's crucial to foster a resilient, healing-oriented mindset.

Equally as important, however, is a practice of mindfulness—a mental state achieved by focusing one's awareness on the present moment while calmly acknowledging and accepting one's feelings, thoughts, and bodily sensations. It sits at the very core of trauma healing by allowing us to fully experience and process our emotions instead of pushing them away or letting them overwhelm us.

The body, too, holds a significant role in trauma healing. Trauma is not just a psychological phenomenon—it encompasses physiological changes, too. Our bodies often carry physical manifestations of trauma, whether through chronic pain, tension, or even disease. Therefore, therapies that involve the body, such as somatic or sensorimotor therapies, can support trauma healing.

Techniques such as yoga, breathwork, dance, or any form of movement can help release trauma stored in the body and facilitate a deeper connection between our physical bodies and our emotions. By fully engaging with our body's reactions, we can gain a better understanding of our emotional landscape and contribute to our healing process.

Basically, the relationship between the brain, mind, and body when healing from trauma is intrinsically interconnected. It's not just about treating symptoms—it's about treating the whole person. Understanding how these elements interact can help us better comprehend our reactions to trauma and thus, pave the way to personalized healing strategies.

Of course, it's worth noting that each person's journey to healing is unique and depends on myriad variables like the type of trauma, personal resilience, available support, and individual physical, emotional, and mental constitution. So, it's completely okay if your healing path doesn't look like anyone else's. You're forging your own path, at your own pace.

One thing is bound to stand clear—when we engage all aspects of our being in the process—brain, mind, and body—we increase our chances of successful healing. We deliver a united front against the impact of trauma, claiming our lives back in full stride. This integrated approach to healing equips us not just to survive, but to thrive despite our past traumatic experiences.

So, as you bravely face your journey to healing, keep in mind the importance of holistic care. Listen to your mind's thoughts, your brain's signals, and your body's sensations. Acknowledge each reaction, each emotion, and each memory; they all bear significance to your healing. There's strength in unity, and that rings true within our own beings, too.

In the coming chapters, we'll explore formal therapy techniques like Cognitive Behavior Therapy (CBT) and Eye Movement Desensitization and Reprocessing (EMDR), which play significant roles in psychological healing. We'll also delve into straightforward self-help techniques so you can kick start your healing journey with tools readily accessible to you.

Remember, the aim is not to erase the traumatic experiences but to process them adequately, to break free from their clutches. The emphasis is on empowerment and reclaiming your life from the shadows of trauma. Because, while trauma may be part of your story, it doesn't define you. You are more than your trauma, and you are powerful enough to rise above it.

# Formal Therapy Techniques

As we unravel the unyielding grip of trauma, let our journey take us to the world of formal therapy techniques. These models of therapy, under the guidance of a trained professional, offer an organized and structured approach to confronting and healing from trauma. First off, Cognitive Behavior Therapy (CBT) is a widely respected therapeutic procedure aimed at transforming negative thought patterns that compound the impact of trauma. It operates under the understanding that our feelings and behaviors are a direct reflection of our thoughts, and by altering these thought patterns, we can revolutionize our responses to traumatic reminders. Then, there's Eye Movement Desensitization and Reprocessing (EMDR), a ground-breaking therapy that utilizes the bio-mechanism of rapid eye movement to diminish the emotional intensity of traumatic memories. EMDR serves to unlock and rescript these distressing memories, replacing them with constructive narratives that empower you. One shouldn't see these formal therapy techniques as a one-size-fits-all solution. Each has its own unique strength, and the most effective therapeutic journey often combines different approaches tailored to your unique circumstances.

Remember, the path may be challenging, but you already possess the courage to face it, and these tools can guide you towards a healthier, happier future.

# Cognitive Behavior Therapy (CBT)

Iis a well-established, effective treatment for a wide range of traumas. It provides a systematic method to confront and modify the destructive thought patterns which often underpin trauma. By challenging negative thought patterns, CBT helps to break the cycle of trauma. These therapy sessions focus on the present, equipping you with skills to manage distressing symptoms. CBT is structured, goal-oriented, and emphasizes collaboration between you and your therapist. As challenging as it may be to face these distressing thoughts, imagine breaking free from the reliving of your trauma and embarking on a path toward healing.

CBT emphasizes active strategies to manage trauma responses. This form of therapy facilitates the examination of negative thought processes that, left unchecked, create a debilitating 'feedback loop' of trauma. In therapy sessions, you would learn to identify these negative thoughts that can trigger traumatic responses. Then, you'd work together with the therapist to replace them with healthier cognitions. It's not a process of masking or suppressing thoughts, but transforming them to trigger different, more positive responses.

It's important to mention that CBT is not a one-size-fits-all treatment; it needs to be tailored according to the person's needs and the nature of the trauma. This treatment requires your active participation, but you are not alone in this journey. Your therapist will not only be your collaborator, empowering you with tools and techniques, but also your cheerleader, celebrating each small victory with you. By releasing the grip of traumatizing thoughts and developing healthier cognitive patterns, you can significantly improve your quality of life and reignite hope for the future. Remember, the step you take towards healing is not merely for survival, but for a life of thriving and discovery.

# Eye Movement Desensitization and Reprocessing (EMDR)

materializes as one of the most effective ways to "defeat" the trauma that is deeply rooted within you. Refined over years, the EMDR therapy process uses a complex, but easily follow-able method designed to sensitize and reprocess traumatic memories. It manipulates the way most significant moments of anxiety are stored in your brain, dissociating the 'terror' connection, and thus, conquering the debilitating fear associated with these memories.

In simple terms, EMDR operates on the premise that your eyes' natural movement can unlock the memory network inside your mind and assist with processing distressing recollections. By following a therapist's finger as it moves from side to side, or the use of electronic stimuli that generates a similar effect, you might be surprised to find the vividness and emotional intensity of your traumatic memories significantly reduced. To say it's akin to physically deleting parts of a computer's hardware doesn't quite cut it; it's more of defragging your mind's hard drive — reorganizing thoughts, rearranging memory associations, and putting all those broken pieces back together in an orderly, useful manner.

Think of EMDR as cracking open the protective shell you've put around your traumatic experiences, altering the way your brain processes and understands them. You're not changing literal memories, but transposing the way you perceive them, upgrading from victim to victor. It is perfectly normal to feel skeptical or anxious about trying a new therapy, especially one that operates in a way that is still largely enigmatic. However, EMDR is widely recognized by psychologists worldwide and has been proven useful countless times. Fears are natural, but remember, it's okay to explore unknown therapeutic paths. What's not okay is unceremoniously accepting the life you're living right now if it's dominated by trauma. EMDR offers you a chance at liberation, a way of conquering the chains of the past to reclaim your future.

## Simple Self-Help Techniques

Often, the journey to reclaiming one's life after trauma can feel both vast and vaguely defined. It's where the simplest self-help techniques play the most effective role. They can create the structure in the healing process and provide comfort in the chaos. These techniques don't require formal therapy or professional intervention, but rather they offer something equally powerful; the affirmation that you are capable of initiating your healing from the comfort of your home. Start with mindfulness; it's the art of being in the present moment with full awareness and without judgment. Sitting quietly, focusing on your breath, and being aware of your thoughts without getting caught up in them can have profoundly healing effects. Journaling is also an incredible tool. Writing down your thoughts, fears, and hopes can help you express what needs expression and bring to light what might be keeping you bound. And don't shy away from spiritual paths that may provide solace. Whether it's meditating on scriptures or simply finding comfort in the quiet of nature, embrace what brings you peace. These are but a few of the self-help techniques that can aid in your healing journey. They're not designed as quick fixes, rather as steady, enduring investments in your wellbeing. Remember, healing is not about erasing what happened, but harnessing the strength to navigate its effects. And the greatest power you have, is the power to take that first step forward, on your own terms.

## Trauma Healing Through Mindfulness

taps into the power of the present moment as a means of alleviating traumatic stress. Research reflects that mindfulness—non-judgmental awareness of our thoughts, emotions, sensations, and surrounding environment—can reduce symptoms of trauma, spark positive change, and ultimately pave the route towards healing. Mindfulness has its roots in Buddhism but is secular in its application, making it accessible to all individuals regardless of their beliefs.

Deploying mindfulness as a tool for trauma healing places emphasis on acknowledging your emotions and feelings rather than suppressing them. When you're mindful, you allow yourself to sit with these emotions without judgment or reaction, noting their existence and seeing them for what they really are—ephemeral states that come and go. By doing so, mindfulness helps disconnect the power trauma holds over your emotional responses, enabling you to react more calmly and objectively to triggers that might once have set off feelings of fear or anxiety.

Integrating mindfulness into your healing process doesn't have to be challenging. Begin with simple mindfulness exercises, like mindful breathing or meditation, emphasizing the quality of your breath, the rise and fall of your chest, and the sensation of air entering and leaving your body. Incorporate these mindful moments into your daily life—when eating, walking, or even while performing mundane tasks. Over time, you may discover a newfound capacity to remain present, feel your feelings without getting overwhelmed, and reclaim the power trauma once had over your mind. Remember, mindfulness doesn't promise immediate peace. Instead, it provides a path, an ongoing journey towards acceptance and healing.

## Trauma Recovery with Journaling

is an immersive, self-led exercise to heal from trauma. Engaging in journaling can provide a safe, cathartic outlet for expression and an opportunity to chronicle your journey towards recovery, victory, and self-discovery. Just as defining trauma and seeking to understand its impact can create a foundation for recovery, the therapeutic act of journaling provides texture to this foundation, helping to build a solid structure of healing.

The act of writing slows the mind, encouraging it to engage more in-depth with thoughts, emotions, and feelings. Capturing your emotions in writing moves them from the abstract realm of your mind into the tangible world. This transforms your trauma narrative into something you can read, analyze, and reframe.

Journaling need not be a complicated process. A simple notepad or diary can suffice. Some prefer digital methods, such as typing on a laptop or using apps designed for journaling. What's important is to create a space where you can express your thoughts and feelings honestly and without fear of judgment. Developing a daily habit is beneficial, but don't burden yourself with set rules. Write as much or as little, as often or as seldom as you feel compelled.

Your journal becomes a repository for your feelings and emotions, showing them as they are, without filters. This process, while somber at times, is crucial. It can help you recognize and validate your emotions and feelings. It aids you in understanding that there's nothing 'wrong' with such emotions. They are natural responses to unnatural, traumatic experiences.

Over time, as you write, you'll begin to see patterns, triggers, or trends in your reactions to various situations. This understanding works as a roadmap, guiding your journey through recovery. It highlights areas you need extra help with and reveals the progress you're making. It can often be far more than you realize.

At times, the act of writing may trigger discomfort or amplify negative feelings. It's okay. If you feel overwhelmed, take a break. You're in control. Know that you can also reach out to mental health professionals, friends, or family members when you need support. Remember: this is your journey. It may be challenging at times but also rewarding.

As you continue to journal, you'll also discover another aspect of this healing tool - as a power-filled practice of mindfulness. Journaling encourages active engagement with the present moment, with your thoughts and feelings, your physical sensations, and your environment. It promotes the acceptance of reality, the good and the bad, creating an intimate awareness that can be incredibly healing.

Beyond catharsis and insight, your journal becomes a testament to your resilience and strength. It serves as a tangible reminder of where you've been and how far you have come. It's proof of your endurance and determination, and a beacon of hope for future challenges. You'll find motivation in your victories, however small, and inspiration to continue onwards.

In the journey of trauma recovery, journaling can be a profound tool. It provides a space for reflection, introspection, and growth that can catalyze healing. As you fill the pages, you're building a narrative of transcendence, a tale of resilience and struggle, and the culminating triumph of hope over despair. Every line, every word is another step towards reclaiming your life and nurturing your wholeness.

# Scriptural Meditation and Trauma Healing

continues the discussion on proven strategies for healing trauma. In particular, this portion of the text will focus on the beneficial effects of intertwining mental discipline and spiritual faith in recovering from traumatic events. The unique combination of meditation and Scripture reading serves as a powerful tool to induce mental calm and promote spiritual strength.

The term meditation can initially seem a bit intimidating. Often, it's associated with monks on mountaintops or those with deep backgrounds in Eastern religious traditions. However, meditation in its simplest form is merely the act of quieting your mind, focusing your thoughts, and allowing yourself to be fully present in the moment. Combined with a Scripture reading or a spiritual prayer, meditation takes a deeper, more spiritually-inclined turn.

Scripture meditation involves focusing your thoughts on a specific biblical scripture or passage. It is an active process where you engage the mind to understand the spiritual message, imagine its practical application, and absorb its divine wisdom. Its main purpose is to enhance spiritual understanding, attain mental clarity, and strengthen emotional resilience.

Healing from trauma is a multifaceted process. While professional therapy and self-help techniques serve as pillars of recovery, integrating spirituality adds a profound depth to it. Trauma not only disrupts the mind and body but can also cast a shadow over the spirit, leaving a person feeling disconnected and alone.

Scriptural meditation can be seen as tool for restoring this spiritual equilibrium. By focusing your mind on divine messages of hope, patience, and resilience, you begin to view your experiences in a broader context. You reconnect with your higher self, allowing for your spirit to heal and rejuvenate.

Yet how does one begin such a process of Scripture meditation? First, choose a quiet location where you can be undisturbed for around 20-30 minutes. Comfort is key, so ensure your position—whether seated or lying down— is one in which you will feel at ease. Then, select a scripture or passage that resonates with your current emotions or situations.

As you meditate, slowly read and reread the selected words. Allow their meaning to wash over you, savoring the layer of wisdom they carry. Focus on each word, what it signifies, and how it relates to your life and your healing. Invite these truths into your heart and allow them to become a part of your worldview.

Is every meditation session going to be an enlightening experience? Probably not, and that's perfectly normal. The aim isn't to seek instant transformation but to engage gradually with the wisdom scriptures hold, and over time the effects will become apparent. It will nurture your mental health, heal your emotional wounds and invigorate your spiritual life.

Many survivors of trauma have reported that their turning point in recovery came when they actively incorporated their spirituality into the healing process. The power of Scripture meditation lies in its ability to provide comfort, bring about perspective-shifts, and galvanize faith in your healing journey.

To further facilitate your practice, consider maintaining a journal to record thoughts, feelings or insights that arise during or after meditation. This introspective practice, along with scriptural meditation, can elucidate patterns, trigger points and progress in your healing.

Scriptural meditation is not meant to replace professional psychological help or other self-help techniques. It's intended as an auxiliary tool that complements these modes of recovery. A faith-infused practice like this could be the missing piece to help you fully embrace and integrate the trauma narrative within your personal life story.

Embracing scriptural meditation may initially seem challenging, particularly during times of mental and emotional pain. Yet, as you persist in your practice, a gentle transformation begins to unfold. Hope rekindles, resilience strengthens, and belief in the possibility of a triumphant future solidifies.

What's remarkable about scriptural meditation is its accessibility. It doesn't require any special equipment or a secluded setting. All you need is some undisturbed time, a comforting place, and a passage of Scripture that touches you. So, why not give it a try? You may just find it to be the key to unlocking new levels of healing, forgiveness, and self-love.

In summary, while physical wounds undergo a healing process, emotional injuries due to trauma need their own healing regimen. A powerful and accessible tool to explore is scriptural meditation, which nurtures your soul along with your mind and body, helping you heal wholly and attain a hitherto unexplored dimension of healing.

# Chapter 5: Rebuilding Your Life After Trauma

Having navigated the strange sea of hurt and dissociation, we find ourselves on a new shore—rebuilding our lives after trauma. It's like assembling scattered pieces of shattered glass and restoring it into a beautiful mosaic. This is where you learn to trust again because trust forms the base of our connections. It means opening yourself up to vulnerability, embracing the possibility of getting hurt, and yet daring to trust, one small step at a time. Your foundation is shifting from isolation to restoration by building healthy relationships. These aren't just familial or informal ones; it extends to our colleagues and supervisors, painting each social interaction as an opportunity to heal. Returning to professional life may seem daunting as it pokes on your caches of strength. But remember, it's not merely about resuming routines but about engaging in a workspace with a renewed perspective. This rebuilt life encompasses healing your self-image as well. It's about standing in front of mirror and sloughing off your critical reflection that unstitches your worth. It means embracing your resilience, acknowledging the extraordinary individual staring back in the mirror, the one who navigated the stormy sea of trauma with courage and fortitude.

This chapter is a roadmap to reconstruct your shattered life, lending you a hammer and nails so you can rebuild it with strength and grace.

# Learning to Trust Again

One of the many aftershocks that trauma leaves in its wake is the erosion of trust. Shattered by experiences that have brought pain, insecurity, and turmoil, trust can be a hard thing to rebuild. However, learning to trust again is pivotal when we are to make headway in our journey towards healing.

Trust isn't easy, to begin with. After a traumatic event, this delicate fabric of faith can be further frayed. It's important to acknowledge this struggle without guilt or self-judgment; take the time you need to slowly engage with the process of healing.

Often after trauma, we can start using our discomfort or fear as a protective shield, preventing us from trusting. Yet, this protective instinct might also form walls that keep out the potential for positive and nurturing relationships. It can create a world defined by the past trauma, instead of embracing the possibility of a hopeful, new future.

The path to regain trust, like all aspects of healing, begins from within. One important aspect of this inner journey is learning to trust yourself. Understanding that you have the ability to make good choices is critical on the road to recovery. Learning self-trust can refocus our instinctual fight or fight reactions, teaching us to believe in our ability to handle situations that may seem threatening.

Start small. Learn to trust in yourself by making small decisions and observing your ability to accomplish them successfully. This can be as simple as setting up a daily routine and following it through. The key here is consistency; maintaining a habit or accomplishing an objective reinforces your belief in your ability.

A major part of self-trust is also learning to trust your feelings and instincts again. Trauma often disrupts our ability to listen to what our body needs. It's essential to reconnect with our emotions and instincts and understand that they hold wisdom and power. Allow yourself to feel emotions, the good and the bad, and use them constructively. This, in itself, is an act of self-trust.

While you build trust within yourself, it's equally important to understand that it's okay to trust others. However, this does not mean that you open yourself up to everything and everyone. Trust is primarily about discernment. Can you learn to identify and connect with trustworthy individuals while maintaining your boundaries? It isn't about absolute trust but rather about sound judgment.

An effective technique to improve discernment is to slow down and observe - take time to know people before you trust them with your vulnerability. Listen to your instincts and check if a person's actions align with their words, as consistency in behavior often indicates reliability. Being intentional about who you let into your life can be a significant aspect of rebuilding trust.

An essential point to remember is that everyone makes mistakes and not to let this shake your entire trust structure. Dealing with disappointment is part of the process. Acknowledge the hurt without letting one incident stall your progress. It's okay to reassess, set stricter boundaries, or decide to withdraw trust, but remember, this does not mean you stop trusting altogether.

Seeking professional help through therapy can also be a transformative experience in learning to trust again. Therapists provide a safe space where you can discuss and explore your fears and beliefs. In this process, they can guide you towards understanding and exercising trust healthily.

Lastly, compassion plays a noteworthy role in this journey. Forgiveness, both towards oneself and others, can release the hold that fear and hurt have over us. This isn't about ignoring painful experiences but acknowledging them and deciding to move forward.

Remember, the process of learning to trust again is not linear, and at times it will feel like one step forward and two steps back. That's okay. The aim isn't perfection but progress. Each step, however minuscule it may seem, is a move towards a future that is not defined by past trauma but informed by it—providing you with the resilience and strength to trust and open yourself to life's possibilities again.

In all this, understand that rebuilding trust takes time. So give yourself plentiful amounts of patience, kindness, and self-care as you journey through the fragile process of renewing trust. Remember, it's not just about learning to trust others, it's about learning to trust in yourself, in your strength, and in your capacity to heal, grow, and thrive post-trauma.

## Building Healthy Relationships

As we continue our journey of rebuilding life after trauma, one of the significant steps to take involves forging and maintaining healthy relationships. The trauma you've experienced may have unsettled or damaged your interpersonal relationships, trust in others, and capacity to establish new connections. This section provides insights into the process of rebuilding this critical part of your life.

First and foremost, understand that building or reviving relationships is not an overnight process. It's essential to start small and patiently nurture these relationships with consistent actions and open communication. The first step in this process usually involves building a relationship with yourself before relating with others. This means rediscovering who you are, acknowledging your strengths, recognizing your limitations, and developing a sense of self-worth.

Practicing self-love is instrumental in the journey of healing from trauma. It gives you a chance to work on your flaws, forgive yourself for any perceived shortcomings, and embrace the unique individual you are. It's not selfish to prioritize this essential relationship with yourself; it's an integral part of the healing process.

After rebuilding the relationship with yourself, your next focus should be strengthening existing relationships that have been strained or weakened due to trauma. It might be challenging to reopen channels of communication or trust, but remember the value that these relationships hold in your life. Reach out and invest time and energy in restoring these connections, and appreciate the process no matter how hard it may seem initially.

Part of this process involves setting and maintaining healthy boundaries, which is a crucial aspect of any relationship. Clear communication about what you're comfortable with will contribute to stronger and healthier interactions. Nobody wants to feel used, ignored, or disrespected, and rightfully so. Boundaries will help ensure these negative experiences are minimized or eliminated.

Mutual respect forms the backbone of any thriving relationship. It's essential to cultivate an environment where all parties feel valued, understood, and accepted. Respect allows you to honor the individual differences in your relationships, which is a catalyst for growth and mutual understanding.

Forming new relationships could be a daunting task, especially after experiencing trauma, but it is an essential part of leading a fulfilling life. When meeting new people and building new connections, remember to stay true to your authentic self.

Emphasize the importance of open and honest communication in your relationships. This may include speaking about your trauma when you feel comfortable.

Transparency can lead to stronger bonds, as it allows individuals to understand your experiences better and support you accordingly.

Moreover, developing a strong support system is crucial during the healing process. Finding supportive people who understand your journey and provide non-judgmental advice can be incredibly empowering. Remember to offer the same level of understanding and support to others as well.

Consider joining community groups or get involved in activities that interest you to meet like-minded people. Not only do activities offer a distraction from the challenges, but they're an avenue to connect with individuals who may be on similar journeys.

Lastly, let go of destructive relationships that no longer serve your wellbeing. Steer clear from toxic connections – these are characterized by continuous patterns of disrespect, manipulation, and emotional abuse. Focus your energy on positive, uplifting, and nurturing relationships instead.

In conclusion, building healthy relationships post-trauma is a gradual process, replete with its challenges. But with patience, self-love, respect, open communication, and a supportive network, it's achievable and plays a significant role in healing and leading a fulfilling life.

It's okay if the process is challenging or if you make mistakes. The aim is to learn, grow, and develop healthier bonds that enrich your life. Remember, in the grand scheme of things, these relationships will enable you to reclaim the joy and fulfillment that trauma may have taken from you.

As we transition to the next part of our journey, we shall explore how to successfully return to professional life after trauma. The skills and understandings you've gained on building healthy relationships will undoubtedly be of value in this context as well.

## Returning to Professional Life

Emerging from the emotional upheaval of trauma often brings with it the challenge of reacclimating to facets of life that may have been put on hold during healing. Returning to your professional life is often one of these challenges. The task of bouncing back in the workplace requires strength, courage, and considerable preparation.

This upcoming journey may seem daunting, but remember, just as you have worked through your trauma, you can reclaim your place in the professional world, too.

The first and crucial step in returning to your professional life is to acknowledge that you're on an ongoing journey of healing. It's okay not to be perfectly okay yet. The reality is, trauma changes us. Allow yourself space for readjustment, accommodate for days where you might struggle more than others, and most importantly, do not rush the process.

Start by gently reintroducing yourself into your work environment. This could mean easing back into your role, starting with part-time hours, or remotely working if possible. Gradually increase your workload as your comfort and confidence grow. This initial stage should be about re-establishing routines, not stressing about performance.

While you strive to regain footing in your professional life, communication becomes key. If you feel comfortable, talk to your supervisor or Human Resources department about your circumstances. They can offer support by understanding and accommodating your needs, or linking you with appropriate resources such as employee assistance programs. Remember, it's okay to ask for what you need.

At the same time, it's appropriate in some cases to keep personal matters personal. Transparency can be powerful, but there's no obligation to reveal more than what's necessary. Establish healthy boundaries to prevent any unnecessary stress or strain on your professional relationships.

Mindfulness and stress management techniques are your greatest allies during this transition period. Simple techniques such as deep breathing, positive visualization, progressive muscle relaxation, and grounding exercises can provide an anchor during testing times. Consider incorporating these into your daily routine to help cope with any escalating tension or stress.

Your performance will likely fluctuate as you return to work, which can lead to bouts of self-doubt. Remember, you're not just returning to work, you're continuing your healing journey and that takes precedence. It's normal to have good and bad days. Be patient with yourself, you are doing the best you can and that's what counts.

Next, remind yourself of your strengths and achievements. Trauma has a way of diminishing self-worth. Counteract this by regularly acknowledging your accomplishments, however small they may seem. Remember, progress and success are not just measured by leaps and bounds, but also by the slow and steady steps towards healing and recovery.

Balance your professional life with self-care and activities that bring you joy. Whether it's reading a book, strolling through nature, or practicing yoga, ensure to schedule 'me-time' that engages your mind and body positively, while providing respite from work stress.

Additionally, consider seeking professional guidance from a therapist or career counselor. They can provide targeted strategies for coping with work-related stress and anxiety, or even help you explore alternative career paths if you decide your current job is not conducive to your healing process.

If navigating your previous professional realm seems overwhelming or triggers distress, it may be worth considering a career shift. You might discover that the trauma you've experienced opens up new paths of interest. Embracing this change can be a powerful statement of refusing to let trauma dictate your life.

Seeking additional training or education can also be a constructive step. This might entail brushing up on existing skills, or exploring entirely new competencies. It reinstates self-confidence and can prove to be a beneficial distraction from traumatic thoughts.

Remember, it's okay to feel overwhelmed or uncertain. You're learning to navigate a post-trauma world, and that's not easy. Surround yourself with supportive colleagues, seek help when you need it, and keep pushing forward, no matter the pace.

Returning to work post-trauma is not just about fitting back into old routines, but about reaffirming your identity and purpose. Work can be more than an economic necessity. It can drive passion, offer a sense of achievement, foster social connections, and provide a routine that fosters healing. The road back may be challenging, but you are equipped to overcome it just as you have overcome your trauma. Keep believing in yourself, keep celebrating even small successes, and take each day as it comes.

## Healing Your Self-Image

After experiencing trauma, the most harrowing battle can often be the fight within. Negative self-perceptions can erode your confidence, making it difficult to rebuild your life. However, by consciously healing your self-image, you can begin to reclaim your life after trauma.

Your self-image is your internal portrait, your personal perception of who you are. Trauma can warp this portrait, leading you to see yourself through a lens of pain, fear, and shame. It's common to feel that you've lost the person you once were, but it's important to remember that your experience, however harrowing, does not define your worth or your identity.

Begin this healing journey by acknowledging and accepting your feelings. It's normal to feel anger, sadness, or fear in response to your trauma. Suppressing these emotions can actually deepen your sense of despair and self-blame. In accepting your feelings, you offer yourself the empathy and understanding that are the bedrock of self-love.

Create a self-affirmation routine. Using affirmations is one of the most effective ways to transform your self-perception. This routine may consist of reciting positive affirmations about your capabilities, your worth, and your healing. This practice can rewire your mind, helping you exchange negative self-perceptions for more positive ones.

Mindfulness is another technique that can help fix a broken self-image. By continuously bringing your focus to the present moment, you can start to separate your sense of self from your traumatic experiences. Slowly, you'll learn to witness these painful memories without letting them consume your self-perception.

Another key component to healing your self-image is letting go of self-blame. It's common for trauma survivors to blame themselves for their experiences, leading to feelings of guilt and shame. Remember, what happened to you was not your fault. Offering yourself forgiveness can initiate a virtuous cycle of self-love and confidence.

Exercise can also play a significant role in boosting self-image. By connecting to your body and appreciating its strengths, you can start to reframe how you perceive yourself. The endorphins released during exercise can also elevate your mood and spark positivity.

Exploring creativity can further catalyze the healing process. Engaging in artistic activities like painting, writing, or crafting can help you express suppressed emotions, providing a therapeutic outlet for pent-up feelings. Connecting with your creativity can foster self-appreciation and a renewed sense of self-worth.

Reframe your story. Instead of viewing yourself as a victim or survivor, try seeing yourself as a warrior. You have battled a storm and stepped out stronger. Thinking this way fuels self-respect and positively shapes your self-image.

Surrounding yourself with a supportive community is also invaluable. Let your friends and loved ones know what you're going through and allow them to join your healing journey. Their encouragement can help uplift your self-esteem and provide a positive influence on your self-image.

At times, professional help may be necessary. Therapists and counselors can guide you through specific strategies and techniques aimed at repairing a wounded self-image. With their guidance, you can address deep-seated insecurities and replace them with healthier, more affirming beliefs.

It's crucial to remember that healing your self-image won't happen overnight. Healing takes time and patience. There may be times when you stumble, but it's important to learn from those moments and keep pushing onwards. Cultivate patience and tolerance towards yourself and your healing process.

You are not the trauma that happened to you. It's a difficult journey, but by nurturing your self-image, you pave a path towards reclaiming your life. In time, you'll rediscover a stronger, more resilient self.

Remember, healing your self-image is not about returning to who you were before the trauma. It's about allowing your experiences to shape you into someone stronger and wiser, but still unequivocally you. In this healing process, you aren't just rebuilding your life - you're creating a new one, shaped by resilience and bound by inner strength.

# Chapter 6: Staying Undefeated

Perhaps you've come a long way on your journey of trauma recovery, triumphant over your past hurts and pain. It's an incredible feat and you're deserving of each victory, each moment of peace and happiness you've fought so hard to win back. But as you well know, life after trauma isn't just about surviving, it's about thriving. It's essential not only to win your battles but to sustain your victory, to stay undefeated. Instead of merely patching up wounds, we want to armor you against future harm. It all starts with self-care, wholly and unapologetically embracing it as a priority. Trauma leaves our self-image fractured and our esteem low, making it difficult for us to render the same care to ourselves as we would to others. But healing means reclaiming that love and care for yourself, tenderly tending to your needs - mind, body and spirit. Alongside, true healing is amplified when we foster connections. Community and connection are antidotes to the isolation trauma often breeds, fostering a sense of belonging, empathy, and shared experience. Just as a tree survives the harshest storms by bending and not breaking, we too can learn to weather life's challenges by fostering resilience and maintaining an attitude of positivity and gratitude. Interventions, activities, and exercises specifically tailored for trauma survivors can be a powerful tool to help foster this resilience. The memoir of someone who has walked this path and found healing could be the light leading your way. Remember, it's not just about mending what's broken, but fortifying it so it can withstand any storm that comes its way. Staying undefeated doesn't mean you won't face battles, it means you'll emerge from them stronger each time.

# From Surviving to Thriving

One of the most poignant stages of healing from trauma is the shift from merely surviving to actually thriving. It's about moving beyond the struggle of coping, or simply getting through the day, towards an existence filled with joy, meaning, purpose, and fulfillment. This transition doesn't happen overnight and it does not imply that you will never encounter further challenges; instead, it suggests a fundamental change in how you deal with life's ups and downs.

Many people view survival as a state of endurance, a perpetual cycle of battling the symptoms of their trauma. In this state, you might feel perpetually stuck. Thriving, on the other hand, is about growing. To thrive is to flourish, bloom, and develop, despite the harsh conditions. It signifies your ownership of the healing process, as you take charge and actively work towards a more enriched life.

There's no universal roadmap to reach this level of thriving, as everyone's journey is unique. What's comforting to know, however, is that thriving exists beyond the boundaries of survival. So, how do you transit from surviving to thriving? Here are some strategies.

First, acknowledge your journey thus far. Recognize the strength it has taken to survive. Celebrate the progress you've made. No step is too small in this journey. By acknowledging your resilience, you build a foundation of hope and resilience, which will propel you further on your journey.

Next, strive to create something positive out of your experience. This doesn't mean dismissing the pain you've gone through. Instead, it's about channeling that experience into doing something meaningful. It could be mentoring others, advocating for trauma awareness, or simply sharing your story. When you use your suffering as a force for good, you start to reclaim control over your narrative.

Another vital element of this journey is fostering connection. Connection defeats the isolation often wrought by trauma. Forge new friendships, nurture existing relationships, and reach out to support groups. Being around those who provide empathy, understanding, and acceptance can accelerate your transition from surviving to thriving.

Mental and physical self-care are pillars on your path to thriving. Prioritize activities that make you feel good – physically, emotionally, and mentally. Exercise, meditate, read, write, gardening – choose what resonates with you. Caring for your body and mind can hasten your travel from enduring to flourishing.

Don't neglect professional therapy as you move towards thriving. Therapists can provide tools and techniques designed to help you heal and grow further. They can offer insights and strategies to help you manage your symptoms effectively and make steady progress towards a life beyond survival.

Furthermore, seek to engage in experiences that enable you to grow and learn. This can mean pursuing a new hobby, taking a course, or even embarking on a journey. It's about stepping out of your comfort zone, challenging yourself, and discovering new facets of your identity beyond trauma.

Lastly, believe that you can thrive. Remember your feats, challenges you've overcome. You've survived, which means you have the strength within you to thrive. We often underestimate our capabilities, so take a step back to realize that you're much stronger than you think.

Moving from survival to thriving isn't linear or sequential. It is cyclical and iterative; you may have days when you feel you've regressed, but remember, it's all part of the process. Healing isn't about racing to the finish line; it's about acknowledging and accepting your unique journey with all its twists and turns.

The transition from surviving to thriving occurs when you start to harness the power inherent in your resilience, use it as fuel to push boundaries, and begin to reconstruct a life of satisfaction, joy, and fulfillment. It is not the absence of pain or struggle, but rather the ability to live a rich, meaningful life, despite them.

Every triumph and setback, every smile and tear, are all precious chapters in your book of resilience. And remember, no matter where you are on this journey, you're a survivor. And being a survivor means you possess the strength and will to thrive.

# Prioritizing Self-Care

While fostering your resilience and strength after trauma, nothing is quite as crucial as the conscious decision to prioritize your self-care. Remaining undefeated in the face of trauma doesn't only mean healing from past wounds, it also means maintaining constant vigilance over your emotional wellbeing and overall health. Think of self-care as an armor you don daily to protect yourself from adding new traumas, as well as a salve that facilitates continued healing of past ones.

Self-care isn't simply task oriented actions aimed at improving health, but rather a deliberate act to maintain, protect, and improve your overall well-being. At its core, self-care means placing yourself on the top of your priority list. This comes from a profound understanding that healing can only happen when you put your needs first. It is you taking responsibility for your own health and making an active effort to promote and maintain wellness.

Often people misunderstand self-care as a one-time act of treating themselves to an occasional indulgence. However, it's actually a consistent commitment to meet your own physical, emotional, and mental needs. It's not always about luxury; sometimes it's about survival. Its manifestation varies greatly from person to person- what works for one might not work for another. This is why it is crucial to develop a unique self-care routine that best suits your personal needs.

Let's start with physical self-care. When you are reeling under the weight of trauma, it's common to overlook the most fundamental aspect of well-being: physical health. Taking care of your body is a basic self-care strategy that plays a tremendous role in managing trauma symptoms. It's not about a drastic lifestyle overhaul; on the contrary, even small steps can have a powerful impact. Start by nourishing your body with good food, ensuring you get enough sleep, and partaking in regular physical activity.

Try developing a structured sleeping schedule, keeping your bedroom environment serene, and cutting out caffeine and electronics before bed to improve your sleep. Even a brisk walk or a few stretches can make a difference in providing a natural mood boost and reducing anxiety. Physical care is also about knowing your body, listening to what it needs, and seeking professional health care when required.

Next up is emotional self-care. Trauma is an attack on the psyche, leaving emotional wounds that need tender care. Emotional self-care is about acknowledging your feelings, listening to your inner voice, and nurturing your emotional wounds. This can be achieved through activities such as journaling, reading, listening to music, or anything else that allows you to express and process your emotions.

Therapy and counseling are potent tools that provide a safe space for expressing your feelings. Emotional self-care is also about giving yourself permission to feel without judgment, criticism or the need to quickly 'fix' everything. It's okay to not be okay sometimes. Patience and kindness towards oneself are important aspects of emotional self-care.

Spiritual self-care comes into play when connecting with one's higher self or a force greater than the individual. This doesn't necessarily have to be religious, though it can involve prayer or other religious practices for those who find comfort in them. Engaging in activities such as meditation, spending time in nature, or practicing gratitude can all be beneficial. Spiritual self-care helps regain a sense of purpose and instill faith in the journey ahead.

Social self-care involves purposely nurturing relationships that enrich your life and severing ties with toxic relationships that drain your energy. It's essential to surround yourself with a supportive network of friends and family, and leverage this support system as part of your healing process.

Hobbies or pastimes that give you joy are also an integral part of self-care. Engage in activities that make you feel accomplished or more connected with yourself. Be it painting, playing an instrument, gardening, or any activity that offers solace-- these are all forms of self-care. Rekindling your relationship with these activities is part of healing from trauma and moving towards a more enjoyable life.

Moving forward, practice setting up boundaries. Be clear about what you can tolerate and what you find unacceptable. Let your 'No' be respected and considered. This is a fundamental part of self-care, signifying respect for one's own limits and instills confidence.

Remember, the goal is not to create an elaborate, time-consuming routine but to cultivate a rhythm of actions that foster physical, emotional, and spiritual well-being. It's okay to start small. Over time these small habits can accumulate, resulting in lasting effects on your overall well-being. Don't feel guilty for devoting time to self-care: it isn't selfish. It is necessary. It is you saying to yourself, "You matter, you are worth it, and your health is a priority". Embrace self-care as your personal commitment towards building an undefeated life post-trauma.

Lastly, it's important to note that implementing self-care techniques will not erase or invalidate your trauma. Rather, they're a part of your entire healing journey, a crucial aspect of staying undefeated and reclaiming your life. Aknowledge that self-care is an ongoing process and not a destination. As they say, the journey, especially one of healing and transformation, is oftentimes more important than the destination itself.

In summary, Prioritizing self-care isn't an indulgence; it's a necessity. Be consistent with your self-care efforts, even on good days. In doing so, you'll not only be taking a pivotal step in your healing journey, but you'll also be reminding yourself of your worth each day. Always remember: it's not selfish to prioritize self-care. On the contrary, prioritizing self-care is the ultimate act of self-love and respect. Only when you care for yourself can you truly begin to heal and reclaim your life.

# Nurturing Connections

To sustain long-term recovery from trauma and to remain undefeated, cultivating and nurturing connections is essential. Human beings are wired to connect, and the connections we establish with others are vital for our recovery and overall well-being.

Survivors often feel isolated and disconnected following traumatic events. These feelings of separation can exacerbate the symptoms of trauma and make it even more challenging to move forward. Therefore, it's crucial to work on fostering connections with both yourself and other people in your healing journey.

In the tumultuous seas of trauma, reconnection to yourself is your anchor. Spend time understanding what causes your emotional high tides and what leads to calm waters. Recognize your strengths, embrace your vulnerabilities, and respect your boundaries. It isn't about rebuilding the old you but constructing a stronger and more resilient self.

Establish a routine that includes simple activities such as reading, meditating, or taking a walk. Try to recognize your triggers and plan how to handle them safely. You owe it to yourself to build a healthy relationship with yourself, and a robust internal connection forms the foundation for connections with others.

When pursuing connections with others after experiencing trauma, it's vital they be healthy, supportive relationships. It's beneficial to surround yourself with kind, empathetic individuals who understand your journey and respect your struggles.

An essential step is to identify and navigate away from relationships that are toxic or unsupportive. Just as it's crucial to cultivate supportive connections, it's equally essential to identify and avoid damaging relationships that can impede your progress.

An effective way of establishing nurturing connections is through group therapy or support groups. Participating in these groups allows you to engage with others who share similar experiences, understand you, and can offer empathy and support.

Furthermore, connecting with others who've endured similar hardships can provide a sense of hope. Hearing their stories of resilience and survival can inspire you to keep going and reinforces the notion that it's possible to conquer trauma. It also reminds you that you're not alone in your journey.

Connecting with family and friends is another crucial aspect of nurturing connections. By including loved ones in your recovery journey, you can feel grounded and supported. Engaging them can help relieve feelings of isolation and remind you of the love and care that surrounds you.

However, it's essential to communicate openly about your needs during your recovery. Loved ones may want to help but might not know how to do so, and divulging your needs can guide them in providing the kind of support you need.

You can also foster connections by volunteering or participating in community events. By being part of a community, you can experience a sense of belonging and importance. Helping others can be therapeutic, and it can assist in regaining a positive self-image and self-esteem.

Centered in the tumultuous process of healing from trauma is maintaining connections with therapeutic resources. Regular sessions with your therapist can assist you in navigating your feelings and aid in establishing a safe space to express your vulnerabilities.

Nurturing connections also means nurturing connections of the past. Memories and experiences are the ties that hold the fabric of our identity. Acknowledging these ties, honoring the past, and learning from it can aid in reconciling with trauma and foster the path to healing.

To conclude, nurturing connections is an essential aspect of overcoming trauma and staying undefeated. By fostering a healthy relationship with yourself, forming supportive relationships with others, participating in group therapy, and focusing on community engagement, you can enrich your healing processes, remind yourself that you're not fighting alone, and make significant strides in conquering trauma.

Remember, this journey isn't performed in isolation, just as a tree doesn't grow in a void but flourishes within an ecosystem. Like that tree, as a trauma survivor, you're an integral part of a wider community of fighters and healers, each nurturing each other towards growth and resilience.

## Cultivating Gratitude and Positivity

As we continue our journey from surviving trauma to thriving in spite of it, an essential step is cultivating gratitude and positivity. Intrinsically connecting with gratitude and positivity is more than just a sunny disposition or chirping 'everything's fine' in the face of adversity - it's about consciously and deliberately adopting habits and mindsets that uplift your spirits and foster resilience.

Our brains are naturally primed to spot threats; this is a survival mechanism. However, when we've been through trauma, this propensity can often dominate our daily perception, skewing us toward negative thinking. This makes it even more crucial for us to focus on and learn to magnify the positive.

Research has demonstrated that gratitude can have a profound impact on our wellbeing. The act of acknowledging the good things in our lives, no matter how small, can help to shift our mindset from dwelling on negatives and what we lack, to appreciating what we possess. Regular gratitude practice can increase joy, contentment, and resilience, while decreasing feelings of anxiety and depression.

Gratitude goes hand in hand with mindfulness, a concept we have discussed previously. It's about being present in the moment to recognize and appreciate the good things in life. This might involve keeping a gratitude journal, dedicating time each day to write down the things you're grateful for. At first, this might not come naturally – and that's okay. Remember, it's about training your brain to spot and appreciate the positive.

Positivity, like gratitude, is something that we can cultivate deliberately. It doesn't mean seeing the world through rose-colored glasses but choosing to focus on hope, resilience, and possibilities instead of becoming fixated on obstacles, setbacks, and negativity.

Once trauma has touched our lives, it's natural to anticipate the worst so as not to be caught off guard. But the constant habit of expecting negative outcomes can be detrimental to our mental well-being. While it's crucial to acknowledge pain and challenges, you must also allow room for joy, success, and positivity to exist.

Reframing is a powerful tool in learning to foster positivity. Though we cannot always control our circumstances, we can control how we perceive them. Learning to view obstacles as opportunities and challenges as stepping stones can switch our perspective from victimhood to empowered protagonist in our life story.

Engaging in daily positivity exercises can also be beneficial. These exercises might include positive affirmation recitations, envisioning your best possible self, or writing about a positive future. The simplicity of such exercises might seem trivial, but their impact is profound when practiced consistently.

Gratitude and positivity are powerful allies in your journey to thrive post-trauma. They equip you with a healthier perspective that enhances your resilience and encourages forward momentum. For some, these practices can be initially challenging, resembling nothing more than wishful thinking. However, with persistence, the impact becomes evident. The goal isn't to downplay or ignore your pain but to create room for joy, hope, and the recognition of good amidst the challenges.

Balance is key in the journey of healing, and the cultivation of positivity and gratitude offers that equilibrium, providing you with the space to acknowledge your pain and trauma while also appreciating the good, the beautiful and the joyous aspects of life. Adopting this kind of mindset isn't an overnight process; it's an everyday effort of practicing such habits and slowly, you'll start noticing the shift within you.

Gratitude and positivity, when cultivated and rooted deeply within us, can bring about an impressive metamorphosis, a positive cascade effect, permeating all aspects of our lives. The change isn't necessarily extreme or dramatic; it comes subtly, quietly but surely, reshaping our worldview and redefining our approach towards life.

Healing from trauma isn't an easy journey, but every step forward, every effort made, and every victory, no matter how small, deserves acknowledgment. As we bravely travel this road, let us embrace every chance to celebrate our resilience, to reflect upon the beauty that's inherent in life, to express gratitude for the seemingly small blessed moments and to cultivate an invincible positivity that fuels our journey to recovery! Remember, we're not just striving to survive—we're learning to thrive!

# 101 Trauma-Informed Interventions

As a survivor of trauma, staying undefeated is your goal. You've gained insight into trauma, its impact and healing from traumatic experiences in the preceding chapters. Now, let's take a deeper dive into active recovery with 101 trauma-informed interventions. These consist of self-help techniques and therapy-based methodologies that have proven effective in ameliorating the effects of trauma on your psyche and your life.

First, let's stress the importance of a controlled breathing technique. Deep regulated breathing has a calming effect on your body's stress response system. By focusing on controlled inhalation and exhalation, you're able to not just physically relax but also emotionally stabilize. It's a simple, yet incredibly powerful tool in your trauma-informed intervention toolbox.

A therapeutic technique used extensively in trauma recovery is Cognitive Behavioral Therapy (CBT). CBT works on the principle that our thoughts, feelings, and actions are interconnected and can be structured in a supportive mindset. You're guided to recognize and recalibrate negative thought patterns that may have resulted from traumatic encounters.

Echoing the principles of CBT, Eye Movement Desensitization and Reprocessing (EMDR) is another intervention to pay heed to. It's a targeted therapy designed specifically for individuals dealing with PTSD and trauma. It can help reframe traumatic memories, reducing their emotional intensity and making them more manageable.

In the realm of self-help activities, mindfulness has gained significant recognition and acceptance. Being present in your day-to-day life, immersing in your surroundings, consciously savoring food, or deeply engaging in a conversation are acts of mindfulness. It's being aware, shedding the baggage of the past and the worries of the future, and being involved wholeheartedly in the now.

Sometimes, healing comes from the routine and normalcy of your daily life chores. Taking a walk, cooking a meal, gardening, or making your bed can be powerful in grounding you to reality, offering a respite from haunting traumatic memories. These simple tasks create a sense of stability and control, disrupting the cyclical thought patterns trauma often triggers.

Journaling serves as a personal, therapeutic tool in managing trauma. Penning down your thoughts, feelings, reflections can provide clarity, progressively reducing the influence of traumatic experiences. This simple act of articulation fosters a sense of control and order in an otherwise confusing emotional landscape.

An often-underestimated intervention is the act of self-care. It's easy to forget ourselves while battling with trauma. However, prioritizing your own needs is essential in this journey. Taking up a hobby, soaking in a warm bath, binge-watching a favorite TV show, or savoring a beloved dessert can not only rejuvenate you but also provide brief but vital reprieves from the heaviness of trauma.

A proper and consistent sleep schedule is another key intervention in the recovery from trauma. Trauma frequently disrupts sleep patterns, but a regular sleeping routine can stabilize your body clock and boost your emotional and physical resilience.

Engaging in physical activities like yoga, tai chi, or any form of exercise can promote body awareness, renew energy, improve mood, and reduce stress. It's a holistic way of empowering yourself, boosting self-esteem and self-control.

One of the most potent interventions in managing trauma is forming connections. Trauma can make you feel isolated and alone. However, connecting with others battling similar experiences can be extraordinarily cathartic. Seek support groups, participate in discussions, or simply talk to someone you trust. Sharing, listening, empathizing, and supporting creates a sense of togetherness, making you feel seen, heard, and understood.

Finally, engage with the practice of gratitude and positivity. Amid the challenges of healing from trauma, it's often easy to overlook the positive aspects of life. Make it a daily practice to list down things you're grateful for. It may begin with small things, like a good cup of coffee or a sunny day, but eventually, you'll find yourself acknowledging more significant positives. This intervention can gradually shift your mindset, bringing in hope and optimism, enhancing resilience, and cultivating self-confidence.

Remember that healing is a journey, not a destination. These interventions aren't magic solutions but guidance as you navigate through your path towards recovery. Practice patience with yourself. Celebrate your small victories as they come. Each step you take, regardless of how small, is a testament to your strength - a confirmation that you won't be defeated by your past. You're continuously conquering, continuously transforming, and perpetually growing.

Do note that while these interventions provide an arsenal for your journey, professional guidance is irreplaceable. Your path to healing deserves to be respected and understood, and seeking help is not a sign of weakness but bravery. So, if you're facing difficulties in managing your trauma, consider reaching out to a therapist who can guide you with their professional expertise.

And most importantly, always remember, you're not alone in your struggle. You are resilient, strong, and capable of overcoming this. Always keep faith and hope alive as you journey towards healing. Remember, you are more than your trauma, and you are truly undefeated.

1 - 101 trauma-informed interventions : activities, exercises and assignments to move the client and therapy forward  by Curran, Linda A., author

*"Containing over 100 approaches to effectively deal with trauma, this workbook pulls together a wide array of treatments into one concise resource. Equally useful in*

*both group and individual settings, these interventions will provide hope and healing for the client, as well as expand and solidify the professional's expertise".*

visit this link

https://archive.org/details/101traumainforme0000curr

# Activities, Exercises and Assignments

After you've journeyed through understanding trauma, its impact, survivor stories, and proven strategies for healing, it is equally crucial to put learnings into practice. The Activities, Exercises, and Assignments offered in this section serve as concrete, hands-on approaches to further empower your healing journey.

The first activity involves reconnecting with your body. Often, trauma causes disconnection from oneself which manifests physically. Using a technique similar to mindfulness, spend at least ten minutes each day focusing on one part of your body. It could be an area you often feel discomfort or simply an area you'd like to give more attention to. Breathe through this meditation, and permit yourself to explore what sensations arise.

Next, utilize the power of journaling, a tool that has served many trauma survivors well on their healing journey. Aim to write for at least fifteen minutes a day. Initially, you may start off narrating your day, but gradually, as comfort grows, explore your thoughts, feelings, and emotions. Journaling promotes self-awareness and self-compassion, both important for healing.

Music carries a unique healing potential. Construct a "Healing Playlist" composed of songs that uplift, inspire, or soothe you. Choose the music that touches your soul and helps you navigate your emotional landscape. Use this playlist during your daily life or during moments of heightened anxiety or stress.

Another powerful exercise centers around visual therapy. Create a "Vision Board" with pictures, words, and symbols that represent healing, growth, and resilience to you. This visual representation can weather your storms and serve as a reminder of your healing journey and the future you are building.

Exercise the power of imagination. Give yourself five to ten minutes each day to engage in guided or self-directed visualization exercises. Imagine a place where you feel entirely safe and comfortable. This could be an existing place from your memory or an imaginary one. Return to this sanctuary whenever you feel overwhelmed.

An effective enriching activity lies in service to others. Volunteering or helping someone might infuse you with a sense of purpose and connection. Seek out opportunities where you can make a difference. However, remember to respect your own boundaries and not to overextend yourself.

The art of cultivating positivity and gratitude is another potent tool. Make a gratitude jar. Each day, write one thing you're grateful for and put it into the jar. On tough days, when it feels hard to find positives, take out one of your gratitude notes and remind yourself of the good in your life.

The next activity takes advantage of the healing power of nature. Connect with nature in whichever way is accessible to you. Gardening, walking in the park, or simply sitting and observing the outdoors can all have a calming and reconnecting effect.

Lastly, return to self-care. Make a list of activities that nurture and soothe you – a warm bath, reading a good book, having a cup of tea. Remember to check in with this self-care list regularly and commit to practicing at least one self-care activity each day.

An assignment we would leave you with is to establish a routine. It might sound simple, but having a daily routine can provide a sense of control and predictability – something often lost in trauma. Start small and gradually build up your routine as your comfort and confidence grow.

Another assignment might be to join a group or club on a topic of interest to you. This could provide social connections and a sense of belonging, critical to the healing process.

The final assignment is to seek professional help if you feel ready for it. It is a significant step forward, acknowledging that you need support, and reaching out for it. Remember, seeking help signifies strength and resilience, not weakness.

These activities, exercises, and assignments are meant to be a guiding light in your journey towards healing. They aren't a one-size-fits-all solution, so feel free to adapt them to best fit your needs and comfort level. While implementing these practices, remember the key lies in patience, kindness towards oneself, and consistency.

Remember, you are not alone on this path. The journey towards healing can be challenging and profound, but every step forward, no matter how small, is a significant victory. Keep practicing, keep healing, and above all, stay undefeated.

101 trauma-informed interventions : activities, exercises and assignments to move the client and therapy forward
by Curran, Linda A., author
"Containing over 100 approaches to effectively deal with trauma, this workbook pulls together a wide array of treatments into one concise resource. Equally useful in both group and individual settings, these interventions will provide hope and healing for the client, as well as expand and solidify the professional's expertise".
visit this link for exce
https://archive.org/details/101traumainforme0000
curr

# Memoir of Healing from Complex Trauma

When we look back at our journey of healing from trauma, we often reference a significant turning point. For me, this point came with the realization that the trauma I'd been carrying for so long was complex in nature, and required a healing path that recognized this complexity. Let me explain.

I had spent the majority of my adulthood unknowingly carting around an invisible weight. I fancied myself successful, accomplished, and independent. Yet, there were areas of my life where my achievements were tainted by a subtle undercurrent of unease and anxiety. Trusting people was challenging, even in the simplest of interactions. Despite being surrounded by family, friends, and coworkers, I often felt lonely and isolated. I had little understanding of why I felt this way until I began the metamorphic journey of self-discovery.

When I first heard about complex trauma, I was unsure if it applied to me. The term refers to a type of trauma that occurs repeatedly and cumulatively, usually over a period of time and within specific relationships and contexts. Events that seemed normal to me while growing up – emotional neglect, inconsistent parenting, bullying – were indeed traumatic experiences that had left a deep imprint on my psyche.

Recognizing this reality was initially overwhelming. The idea that many of the problems I was dealing with could be rooted in early challenges was tough to accept. As part of the healing process, I slowly embraced the truth, chipping away at the walls I'd built around my past.

One of the first steps involved seeking professional help. My therapist, a trained professional who specialized in complex trauma, introduced me to cognitive behavior therapy (CBT) and eye movement desensitization and reprocessing (EMDR). These therapies were instrumental in helping me understand and process my past experiences and their ongoing effects.

CBT empowered me with strategies to manage and challenge the negative thought patterns engrained in me due to the trauma. Through EMDR, I was able to go deeper into traumatic memories, in a safe and controlled environment, making them less powerful and intrusive. I learned that healing involved revisiting painful parts of my past, not to dwell in them, but to understand, alleviate, and move past them.

In parallel to these therapies, I adopted mindfulness practices to help manage my day-to-day anxiety and ensure I better understood my emotions. Journaling provided an outlet for my thoughts and fears and played a pivotal role in aiding me to express emotions I'd suppressed for years.

I also embarked on the healing journey of self-care, incorporating activities as simple as regular exercise, balanced diet and sufficient sleep in my routine. I learned that helping your body feel good is part of nurturing your mind. Gradually, the moments of peace and tranquility began to outnumber the episodes of anxiety and fear.

Building trust and forging healthy relationships were the other significant aspects of my healing journey. I learned that I could choose whom I wanted to connect with and how deep that connection could be. And most importantly, that it was okay to set boundaries to protect my emotional health.

Healing from complex trauma is not straightforward; it is fraught with challenges, setbacks, and then, triumphs. It is indeed a journey that fluctuates, but mindful navigation yields the gift of resilience and strength. The fear of facing my past transformed over time into an impetus to embrace my present and future with tenacity and zeal.

This journey taught me the art of persistence. It showed me that acknowledging and understanding our trauma is not a sign of weakness, but one of immense courage. I discovered the power of resilience residing in every corner of my heart and soul, ready to be harnessed and used to fuel my healing journey.

Through all this, I've been able to transform wounds into wisdom, and pain into power. This metamorphosis didn't come easy. It required patience, faith, and grit. Yet, the transformation has been worth every obstacle faced, every challenge overcome, and every fear conquered.

Healing from complex trauma is a continual journey, one that I am still on. In sharing my experience, I hope to underscore the power of resilience and the nobility of persistence. It's essential to remember, you are a survivor, a warrior. You can overcome, you can heal, and you can use the experiences of your past to empower your present and future.

The journey to conquer trauma requires courage, intention, and patience. I'm here to tell you that each step, however small, is progress. It is more than possible to turn toxic memories into fuel for positive personal growth and change. Remember, you have the power to redefine your narrative. You hold the pen. The journey may not be easy, but the destination of self-love and acceptance is undoubtedly worth the journey.

1 - 101 trauma-informed interventions : activities, exercises and assignments to move the client and therapy forward by Curran, Linda A., author

"Containing over 100 approaches to effectively deal with trauma, this workbook pulls together a wide array of treatments into one concise resource. Equally useful in both group and individual settings, these interventions will provide hope and healing for the client, as well as expand and solidify the professional's expertise".

visit this link

https://archive.org/details/101traumainforme0000curr

# Conclusion

In conclusion, "Undefeated: Conquer Trauma and Reclaim Your Life" is more than just a book about trauma; it's a powerful testament to the human spirit and the capacity for resilience. This inspiring account takes readers on a journey of growth, strength, and triumph, reminding us that we have the ability to overcome even the most difficult adversities. It serves as a beacon of hope, showing us that there is always a path towards reclaiming our lives and finding inner peace. Whether you have personally experienced trauma or simply seek inspiration, "Undefeated" offers profound insights and guidance for navigating life's challenges.